Casablanca

Casablanca

MY MOROCCAN FOOD

RECIPES FOR MODERN
& TRADITIONAL DISHES

Nargisse Benkabbou

FIREFLY BOOKS

A FIREFLY BOOK

Published by Firefly Books Ltd. 2018

First printing

Publisher Cataloging-in-Publication Data (U.S.)

Library of Congress Control Number: 2018930199

Library and Archives Canada Cataloguing in Publication

Benkabbou, Nargisse, author
 Casablanca : my Moroccan food / Nargisse Benkabbou.
Includes index.
ISBN 978-0-2281-0086-7 (hardcover)
 1. Cooking, Moroccan. 2. Cookbooks. I. Title.
TX725.M88B45 2018   641.5964   C2018-900178-X

Published in the United States by
Firefly Books (U.S.) Inc.
P.O. Box 1338, Ellicott Station
Buffalo, New York 14205

Published in Canada by
Firefly Books Ltd.
50 Staples Avenue, Unit 1
Richmond Hill, Ontario L4B 0A7

Printed in China

To my parents for giving me the love of food, and to Zayd for pushing me to share it with the world.

First published by Mitchell Beazley, a division of Octopus Publishing Group Ltd
Carmelite House
50 Victoria Embankment
London EC4Y 0DZ
Publishing Director Stephanie Jackson; **Art Director** Juliette Norsworthy; **Photographer** Matt Russell; **Illustrator** Grace Helmer; **Copy Editor** Jo Richardson; **Food Stylist** Aya Nishimura; **Prop Stylist** Lydia McPherson; **Senior Production Manager** Peter Hunt; **Endpapers photo credit**: Nessa Gnatoush/Shutterstock

Publisher's note
All recipes have been tested using a convection oven, but temperatures have been provided as per standard ovens. Please adjust cooking temperatures as per manufacturers recommendations, if you are using a convection oven.

The dish featured on the front cover is Chlada Mechouia Bruschetta, and the recipe can be found on page 57.

The ornaments that appear in the front matter and section openers are Berber fibula. Originally worn to fasten garments, these decorative clasps feature traditional symbols & patterns, and are often seen today as decorative elements in jewelry & architecture.

Contents

Introduction

I was born in Brussels to Moroccan parents who are unshakeably attached to their culture and have a gigantic love for food, and although they valued raising my brothers and me in Belgium, they naturally also wanted us to stay connected to our cultural roots. So they used their shared love for food to do just that. It was an obvious choice for them, since in Morocco food is at the center of all social events and celebrations, and eating is regarded as a sacred activity that brings family and friends together.

My love for food and all things Moroccan started at a young age. I grew up very close to my mom and I used to take great pleasure in trying to replicate everything she did, which involved eating everything she ate. Growing up watching my mom cook and eating her food every day gave me the opportunity to see how a cuisine could be both exceedingly alluring and easy to achieve. I learned that Moroccan cooking generally uses widely accessible rather than exotic ingredients, and straightforward as opposed to complex techniques, yet has the ability to create unique and memorable dishes. Although I have spent the largest part of my life outside of Morocco, I feel inherently connected to my country, its warmth, generosity, culture and rituals. I am charmed and deeply touched by the high esteem in which Moroccans hold their customs at a time when the Kingdom is rapidly changing, adjusting to modernity and opening its doors to the rest of the world.

But Moroccan food is more than the food of my childhood. It's the food that I cook and eat constantly. And it's also a precious heritage that was passed on to me. I feel it's my duty to make Moroccan cuisine more accessible and I decided to start my blog, *My Moroccan Food*, to encourage others to bring Moroccan flavors into their kitchen and to reach out to as many people as I could. This cookbook is a warm-hearted and passionate extension of my blog posts.

While I adore my tagines, it's crucial for me to introduce you to a whole range of Moroccan dishes that may not be as popular but are just as full of flavor and convenient to prepare. I also love mixing Moroccan flavors with Western dishes; I think fusion food reflects the world and age we live in, and I find it immensely comforting and incredibly tasty.

For me, Moroccan food is like its country, a place of contrasts where past and future coexist and are undeniably intertwined, and the Moroccan city that perfectly embodies this intriguing blend of modern and traditional is Casablanca. I like to believe that the food in this *Casablanca* cookbook is similar in essence to Casablanca the place: immediately attractive and varied, where we embrace innovation yet take the opportunity to glorify our customs. Some of the recipes in this book are very traditional, while others are the result of my fusion experiments — an honest combination of tradition and modernity, where old meets new. Either way, every single recipe made my taste buds tingle and my stomach joyful.

Nargisse Benkabbou

ESSENTIALS

Ras el hanout

Ras el hanout is a versatile and beautifully fragrant Moroccan blend of spices commonly used in Moroccan cuisine. The origin of this flavorfulxf spice mix dates back many centuries, but we can understand its nature by simply translating its name from the Arabic *ras el hanout*, meaning "top of the shop," which indicates that the spices used for the blend are the finest available in the merchant's shop. The most common traditional Moroccan dish that puts ras el hanout to perfect use is *mrouzia* (*see* page 92), a luscious tagine of lamb cooked in a thick sweet and savoury sauce made from onions, honey, raisins, cinnamon and saffron.

One of the reasons I am obsessed with ras el hanout is because it simply never disappoints me. It literally goes with everything, giving a delicious and aromatic Moroccan kick to any dish. Remarkably, ras el hanout also works amazingly well with some of my favorite baked goods such as my carrot cake (*see* page 207), and I sometimes like to add a teaspoon of ras el hanout to my basic buttercream frosting to bring a subtle Moroccan aroma to my cakes. Ras el hanout certainly has a *je ne sais quoi* that makes all the difference! In Morocco, up to 60 different spices can be used in the blend, which means that the recipe for it differs significantly from one shop to another. Some may include dried rosebuds or fennel seeds, while others use more unusual ingredients such as galangal or licorice root. The recipe that I am sharing with you is very straightforward and easy to prepare, but uses a wide range of ingredients, so don't worry too much if there is a spice or two that you can't get hold of.

Nowadays, you can find ras el hanout blends in most supermarkets. Although some brands offer a beautifully fragrant ras el hanout, there are others that contain mostly cumin and coriander and don't really do justice to this wonderful spice mix. The best way to check if your store-bought ras el hanout is good is to smell it. As soon as you open the pack, you should be captivated by a myriad of aromas, but if not, it probably means that it's less than the best. In that case, try another brand or simply follow my stress-free recipe!

RAS EL HANOUT

✳ Makes about 1 oz ✳

1 teaspoon coriander seeds
1 teaspoon cumin seeds
1 teaspoon black peppercorns
1 teaspoon white peppercorns
1 teaspoon whole cloves
1 teaspoon caraway seeds
1 teaspoon aniseed
1 teaspoon fennel seeds
0.2 oz star anise
0.2 oz cardamom pods
1 teaspoon ground turmeric
2 inch length of cinnamon stick
1 teaspoon dried rose petals
about 12 gratings of a whole nutmeg

✳ Place all the ingredients, except the turmeric, cinnamon stick, dried rose petals and nutmeg, in a large, dry skillet over medium heat and toast for 4–5 minutes until fragrant.

✳ Transfer the toasted spices along with the turmeric, cinnamon stick, dried rose petals and nutmeg to a food processor or a spice or coffee grinder, breaking the cinnamon stick into smaller pieces if necessary to fit into the machine. Pulse or grind until the spices are finely ground.

✳ Pass the ground spice mix through a fine sieve, discarding what's left in the sieve, and transfer the ras el hanout to a clean jar with a tight-fitting lid. Store in a cool, dark, dry place, such as your kitchen cupboard — it will keep for up to 3 years.

PRESERVED LEMONS

✳ Makes 6 ✳

6 lemons
12 teaspoons salt
about ½ cup lemon juice
(from about 3 large lemons)

✳ Cut each lemon in half lengthways, but not all the way through, stopping ¾ inch from the stem. Make another cut perpendicular to the first to make a cross, again stopping ¾ inch from the stem. You will end up with the lemon cut into quarters that are still attached at the stem end.

✳ Fill each cut with ½ teaspoon of salt, then reshape them back into whole lemons.

✳ Take 2 x 27 oz glass jars with tight-fitting lids and make sure they are clean (any trace of oil or fat will prevent the lemons from preserving). Pack the lemons tightly in the jars, as this will help them to release their juices. Divide the lemon juice between the 2 jars, then seal the jars tightly and keep in a cool, dark place, such as your kitchen cupboard, for 1 month, turning the jar upside down once a week to evenly distribute the salt and lemon juice.

✳ After 1 month, transfer the jar to the fridge to store. Once refrigerated, the preserved lemons will keep for up to 1 year.

Preserved lemons

Preserved lemons are lemons stuffed with salt and preserved in lemon juice, and I am so happy that the world has finally become familiar with them! When I moved to London in 2010, it was really challenging to find preserved lemons, so I would always bring some with me from Morocco or go to Middle Eastern grocery shops to buy them. But after just a few years, supermarket aisles started making room for them and this book contains some very good recipes to make the most of them, such as my Roasted Red Bell Pepper & Preserved Lemon Salad with Butter Beans (*see* page 19) or Chicken Mchermel — a classic chicken tagine with preserved lemon and olives (*see* page 118).

Preserved lemons have a unique taste — beautifully fragrant, citrusy and slightly tart. In Morocco, they are usually added to tagines and salads to give a tangy kick to the whole dish. Moroccans like to preserve different varieties of lemon, but my favorite one to preserve is the Meyer lemon — a hybrid between a mandarin and a lemon, which is tangy, soft and sweet at the same time. My cousins and I would always fight over the last preserved Meyer lemon when we were kids; we used to eat them like desserts!

It takes about a month to preserve lemons, but in my opinion, the longer you keep them, the better. After a few months, the peel of the lemons turns a dark brown and becomes so soft that you can just tear it with your fingers. I have some preserved lemons that I have kept for over a year in my fridge, and although they don't look as bright as in their early days, their taste has definitely improved with time. Sometimes a white lacy substance appears on the lemons after a while, but this doesn't mean that their shelf life has expired; just rinse off the white substance and use them as you normally would.

Harissa

Harissa is a North African paste made of red chilies and sweet red bell peppers, garlic, olive oil and salt. Across the region, there are numerous types of harissa. For instance, Tunisians like their harissa with plenty of spices such as caraway and cumin seeds, while Moroccans prefer their harissa more basic without many added spices or other aromatics. Personally, I like to have different kinds of harissa on hand at home so that I can choose what works best with my meal. This would probably explain why harissa is such an important part of my pantry!

In Morocco, harissa is often served on the side, and is rarely added to dishes before being cooked. The key ingredient in making a good harissa is the red chilies, as they give the sauce its legendary spiciness and contribute to its deep red appearance. Feel free to use any kind of red chili when making your harissa, but I highly recommend tasting your chilies to assess how spicy they are and adding them progressively to the rest of the ingredients to make sure that your harissa is not too hot.
I also recommend using gloves when handling the chilies, as they may irritate your skin.

The word "harissa" comes from *herass* in Arabic, which refers to the action of crushing dried chilies, since traditionally the chilies are sun-dried and then crushed with olive oil to create an irresistibly fiery paste. Because in many parts of the world the sun is not always there when you need it, my recipe simply involves roasting the red bell peppers and chilies in the oven and then peeling and chopping them up very finely or roughly puréeing them in a food processor. So making your own harissa is easier than you think. I like to prepare a big batch of my favorite red sauce and share it with family and friends, and a small jar of homemade harissa always makes a tasty gift.

On the opposite page you have three of my go-to harissa recipes. Rose Harissa works beautifully with roasts and baked fish, while Fragrant Harissa is the perfect addition to any bland meal that might need a touch of flavor enhancement. My favorite way to enjoy any kind of harissa is mixed with homemade mayonnaise and served next to a generous portion of hand-cut French fries.

Some of my recipes call for harissa in the ingredients list, and by that I mean any kind of harissa that is available or you prefer, whether it's homemade or store-bought.

Harissa three ways

BASIC HARISSA

2 lb 4 oz red bell peppers (about 8)
1–4 red chilies (any type), depending on how
spicy you want your harissa
7 garlic cloves, peeled and crushed
1 teaspoon salt, or more to taste
olive oil

* Preheat the oven to 340°F (170°C). Line a roasting pan with aluminum foil. Cut the bell peppers and chilies into quarters lengthways, then remove and discard the cores, veins and seeds. Place them, skin-side up, in the lined roasting pan. Roast for about 40 minutes or until the skins of the peppers start to look wrinkly.

* Remove from the oven and leave the peppers and chilies until cool enough to handle, then remove the skins from the peppers and finely chop everything with a knife or use a food processor to pulse to a coarse purée.

* Heat 5 tablespoons of olive oil in a large saucepan over medium heat. Add the roasted pepper mixture and garlic. Reduce the heat to medium-low and leave to simmer, uncovered and stirring occasionally, for 35–45 minutes until the mixture looks darker, all the liquid from the peppers and chilies has evaporated and the mixture has dried out (the only liquid you should see is oil). Taste and season with salt as necessary.

* When your harissa is ready, transfer it to a clean jar with a tight-fitting lid that has some room to spare at the top. Pour in enough olive oil to completely cover the harissa — this acts as a natural preservative and allows you to store the harissa for longer — then seal the jar. Store the harissa in the fridge, where it will keep for up to 1 month. Enjoy with everything!

FRAGRANT HARISSA

* Follow the first step of the Basic Harissa recipe. While the peppers and chilies are roasting, toast 1 tablespoon fennel seeds, 1 tablespoon cumin seeds, 1 tablespoon coriander seeds and 1 tablespoon caraway seeds in a dry skillet over medium heat for about 3 minutes until fragrant. Use a pestle and mortar or a food processor to roughly grind the toasted spices. Continue following the Basic Harissa recipe, and after adding the roasted pepper mixture to the saucepan, add the ground spice mix, 1 tablespoon lemon juice (or more to taste) and stir to combine. Continue with the rest of the recipe for Basic Harissa.

ROSE HARISSA

* Follow the first two steps of the Basic Harissa recipe. In the third step, when adding the roasted pepper mixture to the saucepan, add 3 tablespoons dried rose petals and 1 teaspoon rosewater and stir to combine. Continue with the rest of the recipe for Basic Harissa.

I
STARTERS
TO SHARE

Roasted red bell pepper & preserved lemon salad with butter beans

This salad has everything you could ask for in a Moroccan meal: it's flavorful and fragrant as well as incredibly satisfying. The roasted red bell peppers work beautifully with the scented and sharp flavors of the preserved lemons. I usually prepare it ahead of time and keep it in the fridge, then leave it to come back up to room temperature to serve. Enjoy it as part of a mezze or as a side with Buttermilk Chicken Kebabs (*see* page 123).

4 red bell peppers
14 oz can butter beans, rinsed and drained

Dressing
2 small preserved lemons (2 oz; *see* page 9 for homemade), flesh and rind finely chopped

4 tablespoons olive oil
¼ teaspoon salt, or more to taste
3 garlic cloves, peeled and crushed
1 tablespoon finely chopped flat-leaf parsley,
1½ tablespoons lemon juice

* Preheat the oven to 400°F (200°C).

* Line a roasting pan with aluminum foil and lay the peppers on top. Roast for about 40 minutes until the skins of the peppers start to look wrinkly, flipping them over halfway through the roasting time.

* Remove from the oven, transfer the roasted peppers into a large bowl and leave until cool enough to handle. They may release a certain amount of liquid in the process, so drain and discard it. Peel away the skin of the peppers, then cut them open, remove and discard the cores and seeds and slice the flesh into strips ½ inch wide.

* Mix all the ingredients for the dressing together in a small bowl.

* Toss the pepper strips, butter beans and dressing together in a large bowl. Taste and adjust the seasoning, adding more salt if necessary. Serve at room temperature.

Serrouda — Chickpea dip

Serrouda is a wonderfully versatile chickpea dip/thick soup, which Moroccans enjoy for breakfast, lunch or dinner. I know what you're thinking — so how is it different to hummus? Well, *serrouda* and hummus are distant cousins and contain similar ingredients (mainly chickpeas). But their taste is very different, and *serrouda* has a runnier consistency and is always served warm. I love to top my serving with chopped tomatoes and onion to add some freshness and tang.

1 ¼ cup dried chickpeas,
soaked in water for 12 hours
2 ¾ cups cold water
2 garlic cloves, peeled but left whole
1 teaspoon baking soda
2 tablespoons olive oil, plus extra to garnish
½ teaspoon paprika, plus extra to garnish

½ teaspoon ground cumin, plus extra to garnish
½ teaspoon salt, or more to taste
¼ teaspoon ground black pepper

To serve
2 tomatoes, chopped (optional)
1 onion, finely chopped (optional)
Mkhamer (*see page 174*)

* Drain the chickpeas, rinse and drain again. Place the chickpeas in a large saucepan and cover with the measured water. Add the garlic cloves and baking soda and bring to a boil over high heat. Reduce the heat to low, cover the pan and leave the chickpeas to simmer for 2 hours until they are soft.

* Remove pan from the heat and leave chickpeas to cool for 10 minutes, but don't drain them.

* Transfer the chickpeas and garlic and their cooking liquid to a food processor. Add the olive oil, paprika, cumin, salt and pepper and blend until smooth. If the mixture is too thick, gradually add water 2 tablespoons at a time to obtain a thick soup-like consistency, then blend again.

* Serve the dip warm in a shallow dish or bowl with a generous drizzle of olive oil, a sprinkling of paprika and cumin and the chopped tomatoes and onion if desired. Don't forget the bread on the side.

* You can store the dip in a clean airtight container in the fridge for up to 7 days, then warm it up before serving.

Carrot & cucumber ribbons with orange, thyme & black olives

When I was a child, every time I would go back to Morocco to visit my grandmother in the summertime, dinner would start with a bowl of grated cucumber and carrot mixed with orange juice and thyme. This classic, refreshing Moroccan starter may not be very kid friendly, but it's definitely the ideal hors d'oeuvre for warm, sticky days. This deconstructed version of the salad is ready in no time and contains enough chunky olives and walnut bits to make you feel full and satisfied. Once the cucumber ribbons are mixed with the dressing and salt, they will start releasing their liquid, so make sure that you only add them just before serving.

5 oranges
3 large carrots (7 oz)
1 large cucumber (1 lb 2 oz)
3 tablespoons olive oil
1 tablespoon dried thyme
1 teaspoon lemon juice
1 cup drained pitted black olives, chopped
⅔ cup walnuts, roughly chopped
sea salt flakes

* Peel and segment the oranges, then place in the fridge until ready to use.

* Using a vegetable peeler, remove the peel of the carrots and discard, then peel the carrots lengthways into ribbons. Do the same with the cucumber, except when you reach the seeds, turn the cucumber and repeat on the other sides. Discard the seedy core. Set aside.

* Stir the olive oil, thyme and lemon juice together in a small bowl until smooth.

* Just before you are ready to serve, toss the orange segments, carrot and cucumber ribbons, olives, walnuts and dressing together in a large bowl. Lightly sprinkle with sea salt flakes, then serve immediately.

Sweet potato & feta maakouda

We have to take our fried foods seriously because, as we all know, they are not what we should be eating every day. So when we do, it has to count. *Maakouda* is Morocco's finest type of street food, and in the souk or in the middle of the famous Jemaa el-Fnaa Square in Marrakech, you will always have the option to buy a baguette filled with *maakouda* and topped with plenty of harissa sauce. It's usually made with ordinary potatoes and no cheese, but since we've agreed that we are treating ourselves here, sweet potatoes and feta add an enriching dimension. These *maakouda* are crispy on the outside, beautifully creamy on the inside and taste out of this world. Serve them hot as a side, or on their own with a mixed salad.

vegetable oil, for deep-frying
sea salt flakes, to serve (optional)

½ teaspoon salt, or more to taste
¼ teaspoon ground black pepper, or more to taste

Potato cakes
1 lb 2 oz sweet potatoes
½ cup feta cheese, well drained and crumbled
⅓ cup all-purpose flour
3 garlic cloves, peeled and crushed
2 tablespoons finely chopped flat-leaf parsley

Batter
1 teaspoon dried active yeast
1½ cups all-purpose flour
½ teaspoon ground turmeric
½ teaspoon salt
a scant cup of water

* Peel the sweet potatoes and cut into 1 inch chunks. Place in a large saucepan, cover with cold water and bring to a boil over high heat. Reduce the heat to medium-low, cover the pan and simmer for 15 minutes or until a knife slides into the potatoes with ease. Drain the potatoes and leave them to cool — it's important to make sure that they are drained thoroughly here, otherwise the potato cakes will be too soft for deep-frying.

* Transfer the potatoes to a large bowl and use a fork to mash them until smooth. Stir in the remaining ingredients for the potato cakes, then taste and adjust the seasoning, adding more salt and pepper if necessary. Divide the mixture into 12 equal-sized portions and form each portion into a small disc about 2 inches in diameter. Place them on a tray, cover with plastic wrap, then chill in the fridge for 1 hour to firm up. You can keep them in the fridge for up to 2 days.

* Meanwhile, make the batter. In a small bowl, mix the dried yeast with 2 tablespoons warm water using a fork. Leave the yeast to activate for about 5 minutes until the mixture is foamy.

* Mix the flour, turmeric and salt together in a bowl and make a well in the center. Pour the yeast mixture into the well along with the measured water and gradually beat the flour mixture into the liquid with a fork until you have a smooth batter. If necessary, add a couple more tablespoons of water or flour to make sure that the batter has the right consistency — it should be light enough to coat the potato cakes but not too runny, otherwise the batter will break up during the deep-frying process.

Continued on the next page...

* When ready to cook, heat a 2 inch depth of oil for deep-frying in a deep saucepan over medium-high heat until it reaches 350°F (180°C), or until a cube of bread browns in 30 seconds. Line a large plate with paper towel. With the help of 2 large spoons, dip a potato cake into the batter to coat it completely, then quickly and carefully transfer it to the hot oil. You will notice that the *maakouda* will quickly puff up and float to the surface. Fry until the underside is golden, then flip the *maakouda* over and continue frying until both sides are golden and crisp — about 3 minutes in total. Use a slotted spoon to transfer it to the lined plate to drain. Continue until all the *maakouda* are fried.

* Sprinkle with sea salt flakes if desired, then serve immediately.

Charred eggplant & chickpea salad

Scorching eggplant until their mauve skins turn completely black and flaky is an interesting thing to witness, especially when the final result is an incredibly flavorful salad. Francophones refer to burnt eggplant as *caviar d'aubergine* because that's how special and tasty they are. This recipe is one of my family's favorites. My mom usually makes it without the chickpeas, but I find that they work beautifully with the creamy chunks of eggplant and add a pleasing bit of crunch.

3 large eggplant (1 lb 12 oz)

3.5 oz (drained weight) canned chickpeas, rinsed and drained

4 tablespoons olive oil

1 teaspoon paprika

1 teaspoon ground cumin

1 teaspoon ground coriander

½ teaspoon salt, or more to taste

2 tablespoons lemon juice

roughly chopped fresh cilantro leaves, to garnish

* There are two ways to char an eggplant, as follows; choose whichever method suits you best.

* The first way is if you have a gas stovetop: carefully place each eggplant directly over the open flame and roast for 15 minutes, turning occasionally with the aid of tongs until the skin is scorched all over and the flesh feels tender.

* If you don't have a gas stovetop, preheat a griddle on the stovetop over high heat or light a barbecue. Cut each eggplant in half lengthways, stopping 2 inches from the stem end and making sure that you leave the stem end intact. Make another cut perpendicular to the first to make a cross, again making sure that you leave the stem end intact. You will end up with the eggplant cut into quarters that are still attached at the stem end,

which will help the eggplant to cook faster. Place the eggplant on your griddle or on a barbecue rack and chargrill for 25 minutes, turning occasionally until the skin is scorched all over and the flesh feels soft and tender.

* Leave the eggplant to cool, then scoop out their flesh using a large spoon, discarding the skins. Chop the flesh into large chunks and place in a large bowl along with the chickpeas.

* For the dressing, stir the olive oil, paprika, cumin, ground coriander, salt and lemon juice together in a small bowl. Add to the eggplant and chickpeas and toss together. Taste and adjust the seasoning, adding more salt if necessary. Serve at room temperature or cold, garnished with chopped cilantro leaves.

Smoky zaalouk

Zaalouk is my favorite salad–dip hybrid in the entire world. I grew up eating loaves of *khobz* stuffed with creamy *zaalouk*, small patties of *kefta* (*see* page 101) and sometimes a few squeezes of ketchup. This is one of the most iconic Moroccan salads, and every region and every family has its own way of cooking it. Some like it with lots of tomato, while others prefer it very chunky and herby. I like my *zaalouk* creamy, spicy and smoky.
I became familiar with smoked paprika at cookery school and I am so grateful for discovering this flamboyant spice because it gives my *zaalouk* the smokiness I didn't know it was missing. Serve it with grilled meat or fish, or as a spread in a sandwich.

4 tablespoons olive oil

2 large eggplant (1 lb 2 oz), peeled and chopped into 1 inch chunks

4 tomatoes (14 oz), deseeded and chopped into 1 inch chunks

3 garlic cloves, peeled and crushed

2 tablespoons chopped fresh cilantro, plus extra leaves to garnish

1 tablespoon lemon juice

½ tablespoon clear honey

1 teaspoon smoked paprika

¾ teaspoon salt, or more to taste

½ teaspoon ground cumin

½ teaspoon paprika

⅛ teaspoon cayenne pepper, or more to taste (optional)

Khobz, to serve (*see* page 172)

* Heat the olive oil in a medium saucepan and add all the ingredients. Cover the pan and cook over medium-low heat for about 30 minutes until the vegetables are soft, stirring occasionally to make sure that they don't stick to the base of the pan.

* Uncover the pan and crush the vegetables with a potato masher, then leave to cook for about 5 minutes over medium heat, stirring occasionally, until all the liquid has evaporated. Taste and adjust the seasoning, adding salt if necessary.

* Serve warm or cold, garnished with a sprinkling of cilantro, as a side, dip or spread on Khobz.

Madame Wouezna's carrot & green olive salad

Traditionally in Moroccan cooking, carrots are enjoyed on their own, boiled and flavored with lots of fresh herbs, cumin, paprika and olive oil. When my mother left Fes in northeastern Morocco for Belgium, right after she married my father and long before I was born, she was introduced to her neighbor, Madame Wouezna, also a Moroccan but from Tangier on the northern coast. Madame Wouezna shared recipes that my mom had never come across, and this is how she learned that, in Tangier, chopped olives are added to the familiar boiled carrot salad from back home. The great thing about most salad recipes is that they are customizable and have endless possibilities. This is my favorite way to enjoy Madame Wouezna's carrot salad — with pomegranate seeds and ricotta.

1 lb 4 oz carrots, peeled and chopped
into ¾ inch pieces
3 garlic cloves, unpeeled
3 tablespoons fresh cilantro, leaves only
3 tablespoons flat-leaf parsley, leaves only
1 teaspoon paprika
1 teaspoon ground cumin
2 tablespoons white wine vinegar

2 tablespoons olive oil
2 tablespoons pomegranate molasses
1 teaspoon salt
pinch of cayenne pepper
1 cup drained pitted green olives, roughly chopped
3.5 oz pomegranate seeds (from 1 pomegranate)
¼ cup ricotta cheese
⅓ cup toasted flaked almonds

* Place the carrots and garlic cloves in a large saucepan, cover with cold water and bring to a boil over high heat. Reduce the heat to medium-low, cover the pan and simmer for 13 minutes or until the carrots are just tender. Make sure that you don't overcook the carrots — we want to keep them a bit crispy. Drain and rinse under cold water, then drain again.

* Peel and finely chop the garlic cloves, then place in a small bowl. Add the cilantro, parsley, paprika, cumin, vinegar, olive oil, pomegranate molasses, salt and cayenne pepper and mix until smooth.

* Place the cooked carrots, olives and pomegranate seeds in a large serving bowl.

* Drop spoonfuls of the ricotta on to the salad and drizzle with the dressing. Sprinkle with the flaked almonds before serving.

Harissa & maple syrup roasted baby carrots with pistachios

These carrots are a perfect addition to any roasted or grilled dish. I love the combination of spicy harissa with the sweet, woody taste of maple syrup. This meal is proof that ingredients can come from across the globe — Morocco and Canada in this case — and still go together wonderfully. If you can't find baby carrots, just use regular carrots and cut them into halves or quarters so that they are evenly sized.

3 tablespoons maple syrup
3 tablespoons Harissa (any type, *see* page 13)
2 tablespoons olive oil
2 garlic cloves, peeled and crushed
¼ teaspoon salt
1 lb 5 oz baby carrots, peeled
⅓ cup unsalted shelled pistachio nuts, coarsely ground

* Preheat the oven to 430°F (220°C).

* Stir the maple syrup, harissa, olive oil, garlic and salt together in a large bowl. Add the carrots, then toss until well coated in the maple syrup and harissa mixture.

* Spread the carrots out in a roasting pan, cover the pan with aluminum foil and roast for 20 minutes until tender. Remove the foil and cook for a further 10 minutes to allow the carrots to caramelize. Sprinkle with ground pistachios and serve immediately.

Grandma's fava bean & zucchini salad

The fava bean is a special kind of bean. When they're not in season, it is nearly impossible to find them, and when they are finally in season, it somehow feels like a big occasion we should all celebrate. This recipe is my grandma's, which perfectly brings out the deep earthy and nutty flavors of the beans, and in my opinion is the best way to celebrate them. If you use frozen beans, reduce the water to 2 tablespoons because they will release their own juices. I also suggest that you grate the tomato directly into the pan to save on the clean up.

2 tablespoons olive oil, plus extra to serve
1 large tomato, grated
¾ cup fresh cilantro, finely chopped
4 garlic cloves, peeled and chopped
1 teaspoon paprika
½ teaspoon ground cumin
½ teaspoon salt, or more to taste
1¾ cups podded fava beans (about 2 lbs in the pods)
7 oz baby zucchini, halved lengthways
¼ cup water
1 thick lemon slice
lemon wedges, to serve (optional)

* Heat the olive oil in a saucepan over medium heat. Add the tomato, cilantro, garlic, paprika, cumin and salt, stir to combine and cook for 2 minutes.

* Reduce the heat to medium-low and add the fava beans, zucchini, water and lemon slice. Give the contents of the pan a good stir, then bring to a boil over high heat. Cover the pan, reduce the heat to medium-low and leave to simmer gently for about 25 minutes, stirring occasionally, until the zucchini are cooked and the insides of the beans are smooth and creamy. If it looks like there isn't enough liquid in the pan at any point during the cooking process, add a few tablespoons of water.

* When cooked, taste and adjust the seasoning, adding more salt if necessary. Serve warm or cold with a generous drizzle of olive oil and lemon wedges on the side if desired.

Zitoun mchermel — Souk olives

After a hectic day, we all need to relax, unwind and forget about the rest of the world. When I feel this way, I always make sure that I have my "souk olives," as I like to call them, by my side. If you've ever been to Morocco and wandered around the souk, you would have gathered that Moroccans take their olives very seriously. They have their own dedicated area in the souk, where each stand offers different types of brined, dry and seasoned olives. Among all the different batches of olives you will always find *zitoun mchermel*, which translates to "olives marinated in chermoula." They have a distinctive tangy and uniquely Moroccan taste that always reminds me of the intense and alluring buzz of the souk.

⅔ cup pitted black dry olives
⅔ cup drained pitted green olives
⅔ cup drained pitted red-brown olives, such as Kalamata
2 small preserved lemons (2 oz; *see page 9* for homemade), flesh and rind chopped
⅓ cup drained pickles, roughly sliced

½ cup flat-leaf parsley, finely chopped
3 garlic cloves, peeled and crushed
1½ tablespoons lemon juice
1 tablespoon olive oil
2 teaspoons paprika
1 teaspoon ground cumin
¼ teaspoon cayenne pepper

* Mix all the olives, preserved lemons, pickles and parsley together in a large bowl.

* Stir the remaining ingredients together in a small bowl until smooth, then pour over the olive mixture and toss until well coated.

* Transfer to a clean airtight container and keep in the fridge for up to 5 days.

Cumin seed, zucchini & egg salad

I discovered this salad a few years ago, when I was visiting my friend Leila in Oujda,
near the Algerian border. Her mom kindly invited us for dinner and we had a wonderful
time eating and discussing old Moroccan cooking techniques. The dining table was set in
a traditional Moroccan style. At the center sat a large tagine dish encircled with an array of
salads, among which was a cumin and egg salad that was completely new to me.
I loved it so much that I asked her for the recipe and reproduced it as soon as I could —
it's now a classic in our home.

◄────────►

2 eggs
1 teaspoon cumin seeds
1 ½ tablespoons olive oil, plus extra to serve
2 zucchini, about 7 oz each, grated
½ teaspoon salt, or more to taste

To garnish
finely grated zest of 1 lemon
chopped flat-leaf parsley

◄────────►

* Fill a small saucepan halfway with water and
  bring it to a boil over high heat. Carefully lower
  the eggs into the boiling water on a spoon, reduce
  the heat to medium and boil for 12 minutes.
  Remove the eggs with the spoon and place under
  cold running water, then leave to cool.

* Toast the cumin seeds in a dry skillet over
  medium heat for 2 minutes until fragrant. Add
  the olive oil to the pan and then the grated
  zucchini and salt and fry over medium heat,
  stirring frequently, for 5–7 minutes or until soft
  and all their liquid has evaporated.

* Meanwhile, shell the eggs and grate them.
  Add the grated eggs to the zucchini mixture
  and fry, stirring, for 2 minutes. Taste and adjust
  the seasoning, adding more salt if necessary.
  Serve warm or cold, drizzled with olive oil and
  garnished with lemon zest and parsley.

2
VEGETARIAN
DISHES

Baghrir with crème fraîche & chestnut mushrooms

Baghrir is a fluffy Moroccan pancake that is traditionally enjoyed with a syrup made of equal parts melted butter and honey. It is known around the world as "the thousand hole pancake" because as soon as the batter hits the pan, the pancake starts bubbling and lots of tiny holes start appearing. It's without a doubt one of my favorite comfort foods and reaches a whole new level when topped with a crème fraîche and mushroom sauce. But the great thing about *baghrir* is that its batter is neither sweet nor savoury, so you can enjoy it with anything that makes your taste buds happy!

◄———►

Baghrir (makes about 12 pancakes)
1 ½ cups fine semolina
⅓ cup all-purpose flour
1 tablespoon superfine sugar
1 heaped teaspoon dried active yeast
½ teaspoon salt
2 cups warm water
2 teaspoons baking powder
butter, for greasing

Crème fraîche & mushroom sauce (for 12 pancakes)
2 tablespoons unsalted butter
1 lb 12 oz chestnut mushrooms, sliced
2 garlic cloves, peeled and crushed
⅔ cup full-fat crème fraîche
¾ cup Parmesan cheese, finely grated
3 tablespoons chopped flat-leaf parsley, plus extra to garnish
salt and pepper

◄———►

Continued on the next page...

* Place the semolina, flour, sugar, yeast and salt in a blender, add the measured warm water and blend until the batter is perfectly smooth with no lumps. If you don't have a blender, place the ingredients in a large bowl and use a hand-held electric mixer instead. Add the baking powder and blend or whisk again for a few seconds. Leave the batter to stand at room temperature for 30 minutes to allow the yeast to activate and then blend or whisk again for a few seconds.

* Meanwhile, for the mushroom sauce, melt the butter in a skillet over medium heat, add the mushrooms and garlic and cook for about 10 minutes until the mushrooms are soft and all their liquid has evaporated, stirring occasionally.

* Lightly grease a nonstick skillet with butter and place it over medium-high heat. Wait for the skillet to become hot before starting to make the pancakes, otherwise you won't get many holes in your *baghrir*. Pour a ladle of batter onto the hot skillet, and as soon as it hits, it should start bubbling and drying out. Once the *baghrir* is no longer liquid, after about 1 minute, it is ready. Cook on the underside only — never flip a *baghrir*, as you will lose the holes. Remove from the skillet to a warmed plate. Repeat with the remaining batter, piling the pancakes up but placing a sheet of paper towel between each so that they don't stick to each other.

* Stir the crème fraîche, Parmesan and parsley into the mushroom sauce, taste and season with salt and pepper, then simmer for 2 minutes. Scoop immediately on to a warm *baghrir*, top with extra parsley and serve.

Feta & red bell pepper kalinte

Think of *kalinte* as the love child of a giant chickpea and a custardy quiche. I love its intense chickpea flavor and smooth, melt-in-your-mouth consistency. This classic Moroccan street food is usually enjoyed in a baguette sprinkled with paprika and cumin. The name *kalinte* comes from the Spanish word *caliente*, which means "warm," simply because this silky chickpea pie is meant to be enjoyed very hot. If you like the sound of it, you will love my jazzed-up version with feta and red bell pepper — it's truly comforting.

1 teaspoon unsalted butter, plus extra for greasing

1 red bell pepper, cored, deseeded and chopped into ⅓ inch pieces

⅓ cup olive oil

1 egg

1¼ teaspoons salt

2¼ cups water

2 cups chickpea flour (also labelled as gram flour)

½ cup milk (any type)

1 teaspoon baking powder

⅓ cup feta cheese, crumbled

* Preheat the oven to 400°F (200°C). Grease an 8 inch round deep baking pan.

* Melt the butter in a small skillet over medium heat. Add the bell pepper, cover the pan and cook for about 7 minutes until the pepper starts to soften. Remove skillet from the heat and set aside for a few minutes.

* Place the olive oil, egg and salt in a blender and blend for a few seconds until foamy. Then add the measured water and half the chickpea flour and blend until you have a smooth batter. Add the milk, the remaining chickpea flour and the baking powder and blend again until smooth, making sure that there are no lumps. If you don't have a blender, place the ingredients in a large bowl and use a hand-held electric mixer instead.

* Pour the batter into the prepared baking pan and sprinkle the bell pepper and feta on top. The batter will be very runny, but don't worry, it's supposed to be. Carefully place the pan in the oven and bake for 25–30 minutes until golden and the top of the pie feels a bit spongy. Remove from the oven and leave to cool for 5 minutes before serving.

Moroccan eggs Florentine with harissa hollandaise

I love eggs. Fried, scrambled, Benedict or Royale, anything with a runny egg yolk has the potential to make me unreasonably excited. I can't tell you how much I adore my Moroccan take on eggs Florentine with harissa hollandaise! It's interesting how a bit of ras el hanout and harissa can give a unique twist to such a classic dish. It certainly proves that a little goes a long way. The harissa hollandaise is so tasty and easy to prepare, I always make a double batch and use it for poached fish or grilled asparagus the next day.

1 tablespoon olive oil
1 cup spinach leaves
1 tablespoon lemon juice
1 teaspoon ras el hanout (*see* page 9 for homemade)
½ teaspoon salt
oil, for frying the eggs if needed
4 eggs
2 English muffins or 4 slices of bread
1 tablespoon chopped chives, to garnish

Harissa hollandaise
2 egg yolks
1 tablespoon harissa, any type (*see* page 13 for homemade), or more to taste
½ tablespoon lemon juice
½ cup unsalted butter, melted
salt

* Heat the olive oil in a large saucepan over medium heat. Add the spinach, lemon juice, ras el hanout and salt, cover the pan and cook for about 7 minutes until the spinach is soft, stirring occasionally. Uncover the pan and cook for about 5 minutes until all the liquid has evaporated, stirring occasionally. Remove pan from the heat and set aside until ready to serve.

* For the harissa hollandaise, place the egg yolks, harissa and lemon juice in a blender and blend until smooth. With the motor running, pour in the melted butter in a steady stream until a thick sauce forms. Taste the hollandaise and add salt if necessary, then set aside until ready to use. If the hollandaise has set by the time you want to serve, warm it up in a small saucepan.

* Poach or fry your eggs to your liking. Split the muffins and toast them, or toast the slices of bread. Top each warm muffin half or slice of toast with a serving of spinach, an egg and a generous serving of the harissa hollandaise. Garnish with chopped chives and serve immediately.

Root vegetable & prune tagine

For a long time I used to shy away from root vegetables. I somehow found them a bit unexciting. This obviously changed when I went to cookery school, immersed myself in the culinary world and started cooking and eating some of my food pet peeves. If you are unsure how you feel about root vegetables, try this recipe because it will make you fall in love with them. The spices effortlessly bring out all the flavors of the root vegetables, and the prunes add sweetness and intensity to this delicious vegan tagine.

3 tablespoons olive oil
3 large onions, sliced
4 garlic cloves, peeled and crushed
2 cups vegetable stock
1 heaped teaspoon ground turmeric
1 heaped teaspoon ground ginger
¾ teaspoon salt, or more to taste
pinch of saffron threads

11 oz turnips, peeled and cut into 1 inch chunks
11 oz baby potatoes, scrubbed and halved
11 oz celeriac, peeled and cut into 1 inch chunks
11 oz parsnips, peeled and cut into 1 inch chunks
11 oz soft prunes
3 tablespoons clear honey
1 teaspoon ground cinnamon
cilantro leaves, to garnish
crusty bread or couscous, to serve

* Heat the olive oil in a large saucepan over medium heat. Add the onions, cover the pan and cook for about 15 minutes until they are soft and translucent, stirring occasionally.

* Stir in the garlic, stock, turmeric, ginger, salt and saffron. Bring to a boil over high heat, then re-cover the pan, reduce the heat to low and simmer gently for 30 minutes to allow the spices to release their essences.

* Add the turnip chunks to the pan and bring the mixture to a boil over high heat, then re-cover, reduce the heat to medium-low and cook for 10 minutes. Add the potatoes, celeriac and parsnips and give the contents of the pan a good stir. There should be enough liquid in the pan to almost cover the vegetables; if not, pour in just enough water to do so. Bring to a boil over high heat, then re-cover the pan, reduce the heat to medium-low and cook for 20–25 minutes until all the root vegetables are cooked through and soft.

* Meanwhile, place the prunes in a heatproof bowl and pour boiling water over to cover. Leave to soak for 5 minutes until softened, then drain.

* Once the root vegetables are cooked, your tagine is almost ready. Taste the broth and adjust the seasoning, adding more salt if necessary. Remove pan from the heat and use a ladle to transfer ¾ cup of the broth to a small saucepan. Place the pan over medium heat and add the drained prunes, honey and cinnamon. Simmer, uncovered and stirring occasionally, for about 15 minutes until the sauce has thickened and reduced by half.

* Serve the root vegetables warm, topped with the prunes and sauce, and garnished with cilantro. Enjoy with crusty bread or a side of couscous.

Berber breakfast eggs

In my parents' home, eggs are something we used to enjoy almost religiously. They were allowed only for breakfast and never on weekdays. Nevertheless, my brothers and I used to quietly sneak into the kitchen in the afternoon to experiment with highly questionable egg recipes. And by recipes, I mean something that contained way too much butter and ketchup. In my opinion, eggs are much more than a cheap way to have our daily serving of protein; they are delicious, especially when cooked the right way. This Berber recipe is one of the many ways my mom used to prepare eggs for us on weekends.

2 tablespoons olive oil
3 tomatoes, grated
1 green bell pepper (5 oz), cored, deseeded and chopped
1 garlic clove, crushed
2 tablespoons chopped flat-leaf parsley
½ teaspoon paprika
½ teaspoon ground cumin
½ teaspoon ground turmeric
pinch of cayenne pepper

½ teaspoon salt
2 tablespoons water
4 eggs
Khobz, to serve (see page 172)

To garnish
½ red onion, finely chopped
handful of chopped spinach

* Warm up a skillet over medium heat. Add the tomatoes, pepper, garlic, parsley, spices and salt, give it a good stir, then add the water. Cover the pan and leave to cook for 20 minutes, stirring occasionally. If it looks like there is not enough liquid in the pan at any point during the cooking process, add a couple more tablespoons of water.

* Break the eggs straight into the sauce, re-cover the pan and cook for about 5 minutes until the whites are set but the yolks are still runny. Garnish with chopped red onion and spinach and serve immediately with bread.

Butternut squash, eggplant & red onion tagine

This recipe is an old favorite of mine, featuring three of my best-loved vegetables. It's also my go-to meal when I feel like eating something healthy, but it is also very comforting. I usually serve it with a side of couscous, but try it with brown rice or crusty bread if you prefer.

4 tablespoons olive oil
4 large red onions, sliced
4 garlic cloves, peeled and crushed
1⅔ cups vegetable stock
1 teaspoon ground turmeric
1 teaspoon ground ginger
¾ teaspoon salt, or more to taste
½ teaspoon ground coriander
¼ teaspoon ground black pepper

2 large eggplant (1 lb 2 oz), quartered and cut into 1 inch chunks
½ butternut squash (1 lb 5 oz), peeled, deseeded and cut into 1 inch chunks
couscous, brown rice or crusty bread, to serve

To garnish
roughly chopped fresh cilantro leaves
handful of toasted flaked almonds

* Heat the olive oil in a large saucepan over medium heat and add the onions. Cover the pan, reduce the heat to medium-low and leave to cook gently for about 20 minutes, stirring occasionally, or until they are soft and translucent.

* Add the garlic and cook the onions, uncovered and stirring occasionally, for a further 25 minutes or until they are lightly golden.

* Stir in the stock, turmeric, ginger, salt, ground coriander and pepper. Bring to a boil over high heat, then cover the pan, reduce the heat to medium-low and simmer gently for 30 minutes to allow the spices to release their essences.

* Add the eggplant and butternut squash and bring to a boil over high heat, then give the contents of the pan a good stir to distribute the vegetables evenly. There should be enough liquid in the pan to almost cover all the vegetables; if not, pour in just enough water to do so. Re-cover the pan, reduce the heat to medium-low and leave to simmer gently for 20–25 minutes or until all the vegetables are cooked through.

* Once the vegetables are cooked, your tagine is ready. Taste and adjust the seasoning, adding more salt if necessary. Garnish with chopped cilantro leaves and toasted flaked almonds, then serve warm with couscous, brown rice or crusty bread.

Chlada mechouia bruschetta

This recipe (*see* photograph on page 59) perfectly illustrates how a few simple ingredients have the ability to create a real feast for the senses. Back home, my mom grills about 11 lb green bell peppers and tomatoes weekly to make big batches of this salad that last in the fridge for a whole week. My father loves it with the addition of a few chopped chargrilled green chilies to give it some heat. Chargrilling the vegetables is essential to achieve the distinct smoky taste that makes *chlada mechouia* unbelievably special.

4 green bell peppers (1 lb 5 oz)
4 tomatoes (14 oz), not too ripe
3 garlic cloves, peeled and crushed
3 tablespoons olive oil, plus extra for drizzling
½ teaspoon salt, or more to taste
4 slices of bread of your choice,
chargrilled or toasted
4.5 oz drained mozzarella cheese
paprika, to garnish

* Preheat your barbecue or a griddle on the stovetop over high heat.

* Place the bell peppers and tomatoes on your barbecue rack or griddle and chargrill, turning every 4–5 minutes, until the skin on each side is scorched and the flesh is tender. Remove and leave until cool enough to handle.

* Peel away the skin of the peppers and tomatoes. Cut the peppers open and pour off any liquid, then remove and discard the core and seeds and chop the flesh into ¾ inch pieces. Chop the tomatoes into ¾ inch pieces.

* Place the chopped peppers and tomatoes in a large bowl, add the garlic, olive oil and salt and toss gently to combine. Taste and adjust the seasoning, adding more salt if necessary.

* To serve, spoon the pepper and tomato mixture over each slice of warm chargrilled or toasted bread. Tear the mozzarella into pieces and scatter on top, then sprinkle with paprika and drizzle with olive oil if desired.

Aniseed & saffron couscous soup

This soup is so incredibly simple and easy to prepare, you might think there is something missing in the recipe. The musty saffron and the sweet aniseed complement each other beautifully and prove that sometimes just a few ingredients can make all the difference. In Morocco, this soup is typically served at the beginning of the meal during the festivity of Eid el Kabir — one of the holiest religious celebrations in Morocco. Usually, more copious meals will follow, such as *mrouzia* (*see* page 92) or a *mechoui* (*see* page 82), so this soup is the perfect start to an indulgent feast.

2 tablespoons unsalted butter
1 large onion, chopped
3 cups water
2 cups vegetable stock
1 teaspoon ground aniseed
1 teaspoon salt, or more to taste
½ teaspoon ground black pepper
2 generous pinches of saffron threads
1 ⅓ cups couscous
clear honey, to serve (optional)

* Melt the butter in a large saucepan over medium heat. Add the onion, cover the pan and cook for about 7 minutes, stirring occasionally, until soft and translucent.

* Stir in the water, stock, aniseed, salt, pepper and saffron. Bring to a boil over high heat, then re-cover the pan, reduce the heat to medium-low and simmer gently for 30 minutes to allow the spices to release their essences.

* Stir in the couscous and simmer for about 7 minutes or until the couscous is cooked. Taste and adjust the seasoning, adding more salt if necessary. Serve immediately with a light drizzle of honey if desired.

Orange blossom, beet & goat cheese galette

Within the few months of my move to London, I was under the odd but happy impression that every single restaurant I went to had a beet and goat cheese dish on its menu in a variety of forms: salads, toasts and even pizzas. I was thrilled because I love them both separately and together. This recipe (*see* photograph on page 62) is a Moroccan-inspired version of the classic beet and goat cheese combination — fruity, fragrant, creamy and unbelievably simple to realize. Simply unroll your pastry, prepare your topping ingredients, pop in the oven and enjoy this beautifully luscious galette.

1 large orange
7 oz cooked, peeled beet, sliced
1 zucchini (7 oz), sliced
1 tablespoon orange blossom water
3 tablespoons cornstarch
3 tablespoons clear honey

1½ teaspoons salt
11 oz ready-rolled puff pastry sheets
⅔ cup soft goat cheese, roughly crumbled
1 teaspoon dried thyme
1 egg, beaten
salad leaves, to serve

* Preheat the oven to 400°F (200°C). Line a cookie sheet with parchment paper.

* Peel and segment the orange into a bowl, then drain off the juices. Place the orange segments in the fridge until ready to use.

* Mix the beet, zucchini, orange blossom water, cornstarch, honey and salt together in a large bowl.

* Unroll the pastry sheet on to the lined cookie sheet. Arrange the beet and zucchini slices over the pastry, leaving a 2 inch-wide border clear around the edges of the sheet. Reserve any juices left from the beet and zucchini mixture in the bowl.

* Fold the edges of the pastry in toward the center and over the mixture, then press the corners together to seal the galette. Pour any reserved vegetable juices into the center of the galette, making sure that they don't spill over the edges of the pastry. Distribute the orange segments and goat cheese evenly all over the pastry, then sprinkle with thyme. Finally, brush the pastry edges with the beaten egg. Bake for 25–30 minutes or until the pastry is golden brown. Serve warm with salad leaves.

Scented waters

Moroccans mainly use two kinds of scented water: rosewater and orange blossom water. These aromatic waters are obtained by distilling water with fresh rose petals or orange blossom petals. In Morocco, rosewater is used as a flavoring in baking, such as in my Rose & Almond *Ghriba* (*see* page 204), but also as an energizing and refreshing scented water. Traditionally, small silver decanters of rosewater were placed on tables during social gatherings such as weddings so that guests could reinvigorate themselves by dribbling a little on to their hands and faces. Orange blossom water, on the other hand, is mainly reserved for baking and is the favored scented water to flavor cookies such as my Funfetti Gazelle Horns (*see* page 197) .

In traditional Moroccan cuisine, neither of these scented waters are ever used in savoury dishes, but I love them in some of my favorite meals such as my Orange Blossom, Beet & Goat Cheese Galette (*see* opposite and page 61) and my Lemon, Honey, Rose & Swiss Chard Stuffed Bream (*see* page 145). I find that adding a splash of these scented waters gives character to a dish and an indescribable aromatic sweetness.

I often bring back scented waters from Morocco or buy them from Middle Eastern shops in London because I find that the ones sold in supermarkets are overly strong and some even contain alcohol, so do take that into consideration when purchasing your scented waters.

Artichoke, baby potato & preserved lemon tagine

Long before the whole world immersed itself in the vegan trend, I don't think it ever crossed my mind whether my food was vegan or not. To be honest, the majority of the tagines I've eaten all my life have contained either meat or chicken, but I have also regularly gone for meatless options just because that's what I fancied eating. Which is why I love to make a vegan version of this classic tagine — it's so good that no one notices the absence of meat. Depending on the season, it might be hard to find fresh artichokes, so feel free to use frozen ones for this recipe.

10 fresh or ready-prepared frozen globe artichoke bottoms (1 lb 5 oz)

½ lemon

2 tablespoons olive oil

2 large onions, sliced

3 garlic cloves, peeled and crushed

1 teaspoon ground turmeric

1 teaspoon ground ginger

¾ teaspoon salt, or more to taste

¼ teaspoon ground black pepper

1¼ cups vegetable stock

14 oz baby potatoes, scrubbed and halved

2 small preserved lemons (2 oz; see page 9 for homemade), flesh and rind finely chopped

¾ cup frozen peas

⅔ cup drained red-brown olives, such as Kalamata

roughly chopped fresh cilantro, to garnish

crusty bread or couscous, to serve

* If using fresh artichokes, first pull off the outer leaves of each artichoke until you reach the soft, pale petal-like inner leaves. Cut off the soft inner leaves, just above where they join the stem. Using a knife carefully cut off the stem leaving about 1 inch, then pare the stem and base, discarding any thick remnants from the outer leaves. Now, you are left with a hairy artichoke bottom. Use a spoon or a knife to scrape out the fuzzy center. Once the artichoke bottoms are cleaned of any leaves, remnants and hairs, rub a little bit of lemon juice over the artichokes to prevent them from turning brown, then place in the fridge until ready to use. Rinse and drain before using.

* Heat the olive oil in a large saucepan over medium heat. Add the onions, cover the pan and cook for about 10 minutes until they are soft and translucent, stirring occasionally.

* Stir in the garlic, turmeric, ginger, salt, pepper and stock. Bring to a boil over high heat, then re-cover the pan, reduce the heat to medium-low and simmer gently for 30 minutes to create a broth.

* Add the potatoes, artichoke bottoms and preserved lemons and bring to a boil over high heat. Re-cover the pan, reduce the heat to medium-low and simmer gently for 25–30 minutes until the artichoke bottoms and the potatoes are cooked through and soft. There should be enough liquid in the pan to almost cover the artichoke bottoms and potatoes; if not, pour in just enough water to do so.

* Throw in the peas and leave to simmer for about 3 minutes until tender. Taste and adjust the seasoning, adding more salt if necessary. Scatter the tagine with olives and garnish with chopped cilantro, then serve warm with a side of crusty bread or couscous.

Cheese & sweet chermoula eggplant

The eggplant is one of my favorite vegetables, and whether it's roasted, braised or burned, I have rarely been disappointed with an eggplant dish. I find it incredibly creamy once cooked and it literally works with everything. When I am in a rush, my go-to meal is a roasted eggplant because it's so simple and quick, and it always keeps me full and satisfied. But I am the happiest on those lucky days when I have the right ingredients in my fridge to make my sweet chermoula to go with it!

2 large eggplant (1 lb 2 oz)
5 oz mozzarella cheese, thinly sliced
4 tablespoons pine nuts

Sweet chermoula
4 tablespoons olive oil
4 tablespoons clear honey
3 garlic cloves, peeled and crushed
3 tablespoons lemon juice
¾ cup fresh cilantro, finely chopped
3 teaspoons paprika
2 teaspoons ground cumin
1¼ teaspoons salt, or more to taste

* Preheat the oven to 400°F (200°C).

* Stir all the ingredients for the sweet chermoula together in a bowl until smooth.

* Cut the eggplant in half lengthways. Make a few diagonal cuts in the flesh of each half, making sure that you don't pierce the skin of the eggplant. This will allow the eggplant to cook faster and absorb the sweet chermoula. Cover the cut side of each eggplant half with 2–3 tablespoons of the sweet chermoula, then place, cut-side up, on a baking pan.

* Roast the eggplant for about 35 minutes or until they are just cooked. Carefully remove the baking pan from the oven and top each eggplant half with one-quarter of the mozzarella slices and a tablespoon of pine nuts. Roast the eggplant for about a further 10 minutes until they are soft and their tops are golden. Serve immediately.

Bakoula-stuffed Romano peppers with yogurt & hazelnuts

I love *bakoula*, a Moroccan salad traditionally made with mallow. Ever since I moved to London, I have been trying to get hold of some mallow so that I can reproduce my mom's *bakoula* salad. Having failed, I tried using kale and spinach as alternatives, which worked well, but I've found that the closest substitute to mallow is Swiss chard. Used as a filling for Romano peppers and drizzled with yogurt and hazelnuts, my mom's *bakoula* salad reaches a whole new level. It's tangy, crunchy, seriously tasty and yet unbelievably healthy.

4 Romano peppers
⅓ cup blanched hazelnuts
¼ cup Greek yogurt
2 tablespoons lemon juice

Bakoula salad

4 tablespoons olive oil
1 lb 12 oz Swiss chard, stalks removed, leaves cut into strips 1 inch wide
3 tablespoons finely chopped flat-leaf parsley
3 tablespoons finely chopped fresh cilantro
3 tablespoons lemon juice
4 garlic cloves, peeled and crushed
1½ teaspoons paprika
¾ teaspoon ground cumin
½ teaspoon salt, or more to taste

* Preheat the oven to 350°F (180°C).

* Start with roasting the Romano peppers. Use a knife to make a vertical incision 2 inches in length from the stem end towards the other end of each pepper, making sure that you don't cut right to the ends. You will use this incision to scoop out the seeds once the peppers are cooked. Lay the peppers in a roasting pan and roast for about 25 minutes or until their skins look wrinkly and their flesh is soft. Remove from the oven and leave to cool.

* Meanwhile, heat a dry skillet over medium-high heat, add the hazelnuts and toast for about 5 minutes, stirring occasionally, until golden. Leave to cool for a few minutes, then use a food processor or pestle and mortar to coarsely grind the nuts. Set aside until ready to serve.

* To make the *bakoula* salad, heat the olive oil in a large saucepan over medium-low heat. Add the Swiss chard and then stir in the remaining ingredients, cover pan and cook for about 8 minutes until the chard is soft. Uncover the pan and cook for a further 5 minutes or until all the liquid has evaporated, stirring occasionally. Taste and adjust the seasoning, adding more salt if necessary. Remove pan from the heat and set aside until ready to stuff the peppers.

* Once the peppers are cool enough to handle, use a spoon to carefully extract and discard the seeds, making sure that you don't damage the flesh.

* Mix the yogurt and lemon juice together in a small bowl. Divide the *bakoula* salad into quarters and use one-quarter to stuff each Romano pepper. To serve, drizzle the yogurt sauce on to the stuffed peppers and scatter with ground hazelnuts.

3
MEAT

Casablanca couscous

If you get the chance to spend some time in Morocco, ideally in a Moroccan home, and if you hear someone mentioning the word "couscous," they won't be referring to the grains of semolina, but a whole dish made with vegetables and meat cooked in a broth. In most cases, this dish is Casablanca couscous, also known as the iconic seven-vegetable couscous, seven being a lucky number in Moroccan culture and Islam. Fundamental to Moroccan cuisine, it's commonly enjoyed on the national Moroccan holy day, Friday, cooked in large quantities. I recommend keeping the meat in large pieces at the beginning of the recipe, otherwise smaller pieces of meat will only get smaller during the long, slow cooking and you might then struggle to find them in the broth. The trick to making couscous is ensuring that all the vegetables and meat are cooked to the appropriate degree at the end of the process and nothing is overcooked, which means adding the vegetables to the broth at the right time. But if you just follow my recipe, you won't have to worry (*see* photograph on pages 74-5).

———◄►———

2 tablespoons olive oil

1 lb 5 oz boneless beef shin in whole pieces, or any large
cut of boneless stewing beef or lamb

1 large onion, chopped

2 tomatoes, deseeded and chopped into ¾ inch pieces

1½ teaspoons ground turmeric

1½ teaspoons ground ginger

1¼ teaspoons salt, or more to taste

½ teaspoon ground black pepper

generous pinch of saffron threads

2½ cups chicken stock

1 quart water

1 small bunch of fresh cilantro, tied together with kitchen string

1 small cabbage (1 lb 2 oz), quartered through the base

1 large sweet potato (½ lb), peeled and cut into 1 inch wedges

½ lb turnips, peeled and cut into 1 inch wedges

½ lb carrots, peeled, halved lengthways and cut into 2½ inch lengths

14 oz can chickpeas, rinsed and drained

½ lb zucchini, halved lengthways and cut into 2½ inch lengths

½ lb butternut squash, peeled, deseeded and cut into 2 inch pieces

2⅓ cups couscous, cooked according to the packet instructions and
seasoned with a bit of salt and olive oil

———◄►———

* Heat the olive oil in a very large saucepan over medium heat. Add the meat, onion, tomatoes, turmeric, ginger, salt, pepper and saffron and cook for about 10 minutes until the meat is lightly browned, stirring occasionally.

* Pour in the stock and water, add the cilantro bouquet and bring to a boil over high heat. Reduce the heat to medium-low, cover the pan and leave to simmer gently for 1½ hours until the meat starts to soften and just before it's fully cooked. Meanwhile, prepare the vegetables.

* Carefully remove and discard the cilantro, then add the cabbage to the broth and bring to a boil over high heat. Reduce the heat to medium-low, re-cover the pan and simmer for 15 minutes.

* Add the sweet potato, turnips, carrots and chickpeas to the pan. If the vegetables aren't covered with the broth at this stage, give the contents of the pan a good stir to distribute evenly, and if it's still the case, add just enough water to almost cover the vegetables. Bring to a boil over high heat, then re-cover the pan, reduce the heat to medium-low and simmer for about 25 minutes or until all the vegetables and meat are fully cooked.

* Meanwhile, pour a small ladleful of the meat and vegetable broth, about ¾ cup, into a separate saucepan and place over medium heat. Add the zucchini and butternut squash, cover the pan and simmer for 15–20 minutes or until the vegetables are cooked, flipping them over halfway through cooking if necessary. (We cook the zucchini and squash separately because they become very fragile in the process and may break up if they are cooked with the rest of the vegetables.)

* At this stage, your meat and all 7 vegetables should be perfectly cooked and ready to be served. Taste the broth and add more salt if necessary.

* To serve, divide the warm cooked couscous between 6 plates and top with the meat, vegetables, chickpeas and some of the broth to make it moist.

Couscous

In Morocco, the term "couscous" refers to a whole dish usually made of meat and vegetables cooked in a delicious broth, and then served on a bed of steamed semolina granules (also known as "couscous" outside of North Africa). Consequently, for a long time couscous for me didn't mean a side dish or a salad and it was never cooked instantly — quite the opposite in fact.

The word "couscous" comes from the Berber word *keskas*, which refers to the utensil that the couscous is cooked in, known in the West as a couscoussier or couscoussière. Its base is tall, allowing for plenty of vegetables and meat to cook in the broth, and on top of its base sits a steamer for holding the grains of couscous, which enables them to absorb the flavors from the broth. I realize that this process is quite time-consuming and that the majority of you will not own a couscoussier, so, in order to make traditional Moroccan couscous, I recommend using a large saucepan to prepare the broth, and cooking the grains of couscous separately according to the packet instructions.

What is known as "couscous" outside of North Africa is actually called *smida* in Morocco. Traditionally, couscous is made from scratch at home — semolina is sprinkled with water and hand-rolled to create small pellets which are then sprinkled with dry flour to keep them separate. The small pellets are subsequently sifted to obtain small grains, which are either steamed or dried. The truth is I find that fewer and fewer Moroccans are hand-rolling their couscous at home, usually choosing to purchase ready-made dried couscous from a trustworthy source, but they would still never cook the instant variety. However, there are ways of making sure that you obtain the best results from your instant couscous: don't add too much water to the couscous grains and don't overcook them, then fluff up your cooked couscous with a fork and add a drizzle of olive oil to help separate the grains.

In Morocco, the seven-vegetable couscous with meat, also known as the Casablanca Couscous (*see* page 72), is a fundamental dish to Moroccan cuisine, usually cooked in fairly large quantities and served in a communal dish, symbolizing the bringing together of family and friends. I've also given two other recipes for traditional Moroccan couscous: Fes Couscous made with chicken (*see* page 108) and Essaouira Couscous with fish (*see* page 146). In many other recipes, I suggest enjoying your dish with a side of couscous, and by this I mean plain grains of couscous and not couscous in its traditional Moroccan meaning.

Tagine

I have a big family. Actually, "big" is an understatement — I have a gigantic family. My mother has six siblings and my father eleven, each with an average of three children, so feeding everyone during family gatherings can be a challenge. Throughout the years, the approach that has proven most convenient and successful is to make massive pots of tagine.

The traditional earthenware pot and the dish cooked in the pot share the name "tagine." Historically, the nomads of North Africa used this now-famous cooking pot as a portable oven, enabling them to prepare a hot meal at any time while on the move. The base of the tagine pot is wide and shallow, while its lid is conical in shape and seals on to the base. Together, the two components constitute a form of clay oven that was placed over an open fire for cooking. While the food is being cooked, steam rises into the cone, condenses and then falls back down into the dish, keeping the ingredients constantly basted, moist and tender. Traditionally, tagine pots were made of clay, but nowadays they come in different types of material. If you wish to purchase a tagine from the souk in Morocco, I would recommend an unglazed clay pot. Be aware that those designed just for serving food are often beautifully decorated and embellished but can't be exposed to heat.

The question I am often asked is, do I need a tagine pot to make a real Moroccan tagine? My answer is no — modern Moroccans rarely cook homemade tagines in actual tagine pots. However, if you want to use a tagine pot just make sure that you adjust the cooking time — my tagine recipes are designed for regular saucepans so they will cook more slowly in a tagine pot.

There are four main categories of tagine in Morocco, irrespective of whether they contain meat, poultry or fish, and each can be customized with seasonal vegetables, dried fruits, preserved lemons, olives and nuts:

Tagine *mqualli* is cooked in olive oil and seasoned with ground turmeric, ground ginger and saffron threads, and is bright, deep yellow in color — *see* Zucchini, Thyme & Beef Shin Tagine, page 78, and Chicken *Kdra* with Apricots, page 120.

Tagine *mhammer* is cooked in butter and seasoned with paprika and ground cumin, and is a dark brownish red in color — *see* Meat Tagine Mhammer with Baby Potatoes, page 80.

Tagine *mchermel* is seasoned with chermoula (*see* page 142) — *see* Chicken Mchermel, page 118, and Classic Oven-baked Fish Tagine, page 141.

Tagine in tomato sauce speaks for itself and is typically cooked in olive oil and seasoned with ground cumin and paprika — *see* Fragrant Seafood & Tomato Tagine, page 138, and Kefta & Lentil Shakshuka, page 102.

Zucchini, thyme & beef shin tagine

This is an old classic that my grandmother used to make for us during the summer. It's a basic beef tagine to which zucchini and thyme sprigs are added toward the end of cooking. The fresh thyme gives a sweet scented taste to this tagine and makes it totally irresistible. In Morocco, the type of zucchini we use for this recipe is called *slaoui*, which is similar to a summer squash except greener and larger. If you can get hold of them, use them, but otherwise go for baby zucchini or regular ones halved or quartered. I love using beef shin in my tagines for its great melt-in-your-mouth potential. That said, feel free to use any another braising cut of beef or lamb for this recipe. Make sure that you keep the meat in large pieces because you will need to remove it from the saucepan once it's cooked.

2 tablespoons olive oil
3 large onions, sliced
3 garlic cloves, peeled and crushed
2 lb 4 oz boneless beef shin in whole pieces
1 cup vegetable stock
1 teaspoon ground turmeric
1 teaspoon ground ginger

¾ teaspoon salt, or more to taste
¼ teaspoon ground black pepper
7 thyme sprigs
1 lb 12 oz baby zucchini or regular zucchini, halved lengthways and cut into 2½ inch lengths
crusty bread or couscous, to serve

* Heat the olive oil in a large saucepan over medium-low heat. Add the onions, cover the pan and leave to cook for about 15 minutes until they are soft and translucent, stirring occasionally. Then add the garlic and meat and cook for a further 10 minutes or until the meat is lightly browned, turning it occasionally.

* Add the stock, turmeric, ginger, salt and pepper and bring to a boil over high heat. Cover the pan, reduce the heat to medium-low and leave to simmer gently, stirring every now and then, for about 2 hours or until the meat is cooked and fork tender. If it looks like there isn't enough liquid in the pan at any point during the cooking process, add a couple tablespoons of water.

* Use tongs to carefully remove the meat from the pan, leaving the juices in the pan. Cover the meat with aluminum foil to keep it warm and set aside until you are ready to serve.

* Add the thyme sprigs to the pan and throw in the zucchini, re-cover the pan and leave to simmer for 15–20 minutes or until the zucchini are soft, flipping them over halfway through the cooking time if necessary. Taste the sauce and adjust the seasoning, adding more salt if necessary.

* Top the meat with the zucchini and the juices, and serve with crusty bread or couscous.

Meat tagine mhammer with baby potatoes

If the Hungarian *paprikash* was looking for a distant Moroccan cousin, it would definitely be the tagine *mhammer*. In fact, one of this classic Moroccan tagine's main ingredients is paprika, which gives the tagine its irresistible warm pungent taste and dark amber red tone. As with all kinds of tagines, *mhammer* is traditionally served with bread, but I love to make an exception for this one. The slow-cooked and then grilled lamb and rich onion sauce go unbelievably well with baby potatoes. Use large pieces of neck fillet to make sure that you can easily remove them from the pan once cooked.

2¾ tablespoons butter

4 large onions, sliced

2 lb 4 oz lamb or beef neck fillet, cut into large pieces, about 5.5 oz each

4 garlic cloves, peeled and crushed

2 teaspoons paprika

1 teaspoon ground cumin

¾ teaspoon salt, or more to taste

¼ teaspoon ground black pepper

⅛ teaspoon cayenne pepper

1 cup beef stock

1 lb 5 oz baby potatoes, scrubbed

roughly chopped fresh cilantro, to garnish

* Melt the butter in a large saucepan over medium-low heat. Add the onions, cover the pan and cook for about 20 minutes or until they are soft and translucent, stirring occasionally.

* Add the meat, garlic, paprika, cumin, salt, pepper and cayenne and give the contents of the pan a good stir. Pour in the stock and bring to a boil over high heat. Cover the pan, reduce the heat to medium-low and leave to simmer gently, stirring every now and then, for about 2 hours until the meat is fork tender — but make sure that you don't overcook the meat, otherwise it will start to fall apart. If it looks like there isn't enough liquid in the pan at any point during the cooking process, add a few tablespoons of water.

* Use tongs to remove the meat from the pan and set aside. Continue cooking the sauce over medium heat, uncovered, for about 35 minutes until it has reduced by half and becomes thick and jelly-like, stirring occasionally.

* Meanwhile, place the baby potatoes in a separate saucepan, cover with water and bring to a boil over medium-high heat. Reduce the heat to medium-low, cover the pan and simmer for about 15 minutes or until the potatoes are cooked through and tender. Drain the potatoes.

* Preheat your oven broiler to high. When the sauce is nearly ready, arrange the pieces of meat and baby potatoes in a roasting pan, place under the broiler and cook for 3–5 minutes on each side or until the meat and potatoes are golden.

* To serve, immediately transfer the meat and potatoes to a large serving plate, cover the meat with onion sauce and garnish with cilantro.

Mama's harira

Harira is a velvety, chunky soup enjoyed all across Morocco. In its most basic form, it is made using tomatoes, herbs, pulses and meat. Like all the classics of Moroccan cuisine, every region and every family has its own version of *harira*. Some add fish or vermicelli, while others add carrots and rice. One thing that is a constant in all versions is the silky consistency, which I guess explains where its name comes from, since *harir* in Arabic means "silk." This super-comforting texture is obtained by thickening the soup at the end with flour, traditionally all-purpose flour, but my mother (and consequently I) prefer using cornstarch for its lightness. In Morocco, *harira* is customarily enjoyed every day during the month of Ramadan, with families making massive pots of it to feed the whole family and often unexpected guests such as cousins and neighbours. A bowl of *harira* makes a nutrient-packed meal in itself, especially when served alongside fresh figs and dates.

1½ tablespoons olive oil

1 large onion, finely chopped

½ lb boneless stewing beef, such as chuck steak or neck fillet, or lamb, such as shoulder or neck fillet, trimmed of excess fat and cut into 1 inch chunks

2 cups vegetable or chicken stock

2 cups passata

5 oz celery, finely chopped

½ cup flat-leaf parsley, finely chopped

1 tablespoon tomato purée

1¼ teaspoons salt, or more to taste

1 teaspoon ground ginger

½ teaspoon ground turmeric

½ teaspoon ground black pepper

¼ heaped teaspoon ground cinnamon

generous pinch of saffron threads

1 quart water

⅓ cup dried green lentils

4 oz (drained weight) canned chickpeas, rinsed and drained

⅓ cup white long-grain rice

3 tablespoons cornstarch

2 tablespoons chopped fresh cilantro

lemon wedges, to serve

* Heat the olive oil in a large saucepan over medium heat. Add the onion and meat and cook for about 5 minutes, stirring occasionally, until the meat is lightly browned.

* Add the stock, passata, celery, parsley, tomato purée, salt and all the spices, then stir in the measured water. Bring to a boil over high heat, then cover the pan, reduce the heat to low and leave to simmer for 1–1¼ hours, stirring occasionally, until the meat is almost cooked and fork tender.

* Stir in the lentils, re-cover the pan and cook for a further 5 minutes, then add the chickpeas and rice and give the contents of the pan a good stir. Re-cover and cook for another 15 minutes until both the rice and lentils are cooked.

* Mix the cornstarch with 3 tablespoons water in a small bowl until smooth. Add to the soup and stir to combine, then simmer for 5 minutes or until the *harira* thickens. Taste and adjust the seasoning, adding more salt if necessary. Finally, stir in the chopped cilantro and serve immediately with lemon wedges.

My grandfather's mechoui with yogurt & mint sauce

Like his father and his grandfather, my grandfather was a butcher. In turn, my father worked at his father's butcher's shop up until he left for Brussels, where in a way he has perpetuated, together with my brothers, his ancestors' passion for all things meaty. In short, the men in my family take meat and how to choose the best cut for a specific meal extremely seriously. My father and my brothers would all agree that one of their favorite ways to enjoy lamb is *mechoui*, which translates from Arabic to "roasted." Traditionally, a *mechoui* refers to a whole roasted lamb and not just a portion of it, but given that the days when homemakers would routinely prepare enough food to feed 20 people are long gone, we are "just" using a shoulder of lamb and my grandfather's magic *mechoui* rub. My grandfather's shop was in the butcher section of the souk in the old medina of Fes in Morocco, and he would often be expressly asked to prepare the rub for his customers' special events such as birthdays and weddings. That's how good it is! Roast the lamb, then pull the juicy meat apart and enjoy with the sauce and plenty of bread (*see* photograph on pages 84-5).

4.5 lbs lamb shoulder
3 tablespoons ghee
6 garlic cloves, peeled and crushed
1½ teaspoons ground cumin
1½ teaspoons ground ginger
1½ teaspoons ground coriander
1 heaped teaspoon salt
generous pinch of saffron threads
bread, to serve

Yogurt & mint sauce
5 tablespoons Greek yogurt
3 tablespoons mayonnaise
5 mint sprigs, leaves picked and finely chopped
1 tablespoon lemon juice
1 garlic clove, peeled and crushed
1 teaspoon dried mint
salt and pepper

* Preheat the oven to 350°F (180°C). Place the lamb shoulder, skin-side up, in a large roasting pan.

* Mix the ghee, garlic, cumin, ginger, coriander, salt and saffron together in a small bowl until well combined. Using a sharp knife, make small but deep incisions all over the lamb shoulder. Rub the ghee mixture all over the meat, making sure that you work it into the incisions, which will enable the meat to absorb all the flavors of the rub while roasting.

* Cover the pan tightly with aluminum foil and roast the lamb for 3 hours, basting the meat every 45 minutes with the juices in the tray. Lift the foil off and roast the lamb for a further 35–45 minutes or until the skin is crisp and golden and the meat is tender and falling off the bone. Remove the pan from the oven, cover the lamb with foil and leave to rest for 15 minutes.

* While the lamb is roasting, stir all the ingredients for the sauce together in a small bowl until smooth. Taste and adjust the seasoning, adding more salt and pepper as necessary. Cover with plastic wrap and place in the fridge until ready to serve.

* When the lamb has rested, use 2 forks to shred the meat and then serve immediately with the yogurt and mint sauce and plenty of bread on the side.

Mama's khlii

Khlii, a kind of meat confit or jerky, reminds me of Fes in Morocco and my grandparents' gigantic riad with its countless rooms and an almost open ceiling. I spent so many summers over there, and my cousins and my favorite activity was to take the many stairs up to the rooftop, which was like our garden patio back home except that it had a beautiful view of the rest of the city. Occasionally, we would find pieces of *khlii* hanging on the clothes line, and I would always ask my mom what these were and why she had hung them up instead of clothes, and how come we ate them and wasn't it gross that all the flies could land on them. Every time she would explain to me that this was the best way to dry and preserve meat naturally. While those logs of *khlii* were tanning, my cousins and I would invariably play games that involved making a big mess with our water guns, so we had to be careful not to wet the *khlii*. *Khlii* is extremely tasty and is the perfect addition for anything that requires a good kick of flavor such as salads, sandwiches or stews. I grew up in Brussels, which is a wonderful city, but the sun is not always out, therefore drying meat naturally is something my mom could never do successfully there. The one time she tried hanging pieces of meat in our garden to dry, the sun just wasn't strong enough (and I think it really scared our neighbors) — so she decided to dry the meat in the oven instead!

Khlii is traditionally cooked in animal fat and then covered in more animal fat to preserve it, whereas the only fat my mom's *khlii* contains is uncooked olive oil. It's not only healthier this way, but also tastier and lighter than the traditional product. The most common way to eat *khlii* in Morocco is with fried eggs — simply add pieces of *khlii* to a hot skillet and then crack some eggs around the *khlii* and fry until cooked to your liking. Heaven! Alternatively, make a batch of my luscious *Khlii* Scones (*see* page 182).

━━◆━━

3 tablespoons coriander seeds
1½ tablespoons cumin seeds
6 garlic cloves, peeled and crushed
1¼ cups olive oil
1 tablespoon white wine vinegar
1½ teaspoons salt
1 lb 2 oz chuck steak (or any cut of beef for braising), cut into long strips 1 inch wide
1¼ cups water

━━◆━━

Continued on the next page...

* Toast the coriander and cumin seeds in a dry skillet over medium heat for about 2 minutes until fragrant. Transfer to a spice or coffee grinder and pulse or grind until finely ground or grind using a pestle and mortar.

* Mix the ground spices, garlic, 1½ tablespoons of the olive oil, vinegar and salt together in a large bowl to form a paste. Add the strips of beef, then use your hands to massage the meat with the paste, making sure that it is fully coated. Cover the bowl with plastic wrap and leave to marinate in the fridge for 6–24 hours.

* The next step is to dry the meat. Preheat the oven to 230°F (110°C).

* Place a wire rack inside a large roasting pan and arrange the strips of meat on top of the wire rack (using a wire rack helps to speed up the drying process). Transfer the pan to the warm oven and leave to dry for 3–3½ hours until the meat turns black and feels like soft branches of wood — we want the meat to harden yet remain pliable.

* Once the meat is dry, the next step is to cook it in water. Pour the water into a large saucepan and add the strips of beef, if necessary cutting them in half so that they fit in the base of the pan. There should be just enough water to roughly cover the meat; if not, pour in just enough extra water to do so. Bring to a boil over high heat, then reduce the heat to low and leave to simmer gently for 1–1 hour 20 minutes or until all the liquid has evaporated and the meat is more pliable (but not fork tender), carefully flipping the strips over every now and then.

* Transfer the pieces of *khlii* to a container with a tight-fitting lid and cover with the remaining olive oil — this will act as a natural preservative and allow you to keep your *khlii* for longer. Leave to cool before sealing the container and placing in the fridge, where it will keep for up to 1 month.

Sweet chermoula seared beef

Chermoula is a North African condiment used extensively in Moroccan cooking that goes with pretty much everything, including roasted vegetables, barbecued meat and roasts, although in Morocco we mainly use it with fish (*see* page 141). I think of it as a fierce, aromatic version of chimichurri that works like a flavor bomb — a powerful marinade that will add a big boost of flavor to any ingredient. One day I experimented with a sweet version of chermoula with honey and I fell deeply in love with it. If you like this dish, try my Cheese & Sweet Chermoula Eggplant (*see* page 66).

1 recipe quantity Sweet Chermoula (*see* page 66)
2 sirloin steaks (14 oz)
olive oil, for rubbing the steaks
1 shallot, finely chopped
⅔ cup salad leaves

* Place all the ingredients for the sweet chermoula in a bowl and stir together until smooth. Cover with plastic wrap and keep in the fridge until ready to serve.

* Heat a large skillet over high heat and wait for it to become piping hot. Rub a bit of olive oil on both sides of the steaks, add to the hot pan and sear the steaks for 3 minutes on each side. Remove from the pan and leave to rest for a few minutes.

* When ready to serve, slice the steaks into thin slices and arrange them on a large plate, drizzle the sweet chermoula all over the meat and top with finely chopped shallot and salad leaves.

Kebab maghdor

Kebab *maghdor* is potentially what happens when you've planned on having a barbecue party, get the skewers ready and then it starts raining, but you still have to make lunch or dinner. That's because kebab *maghdor* in Arabic means "betrayed kebab," where meat that was supposed to be enjoyed barbecued on skewers ends up being cooked in a tagine or pan. This recipe is a beloved classic in many Moroccan households and is often prepared with leftover kebabs. That said, if you're in the mood for some grilled Moroccan skewers, simply ignore the tagine steps and thread the chunks of meat on to skewers before chargrilling them to your liking.

Beef kebab

1 lb 2 oz grilling steak, such as sirloin or filet mignon, cut into 1 inch chunks

2 large red onions, very finely chopped

½ cup fresh cilantro, very finely chopped

½ cup flat-leaf parsley, very finely chopped

½ teaspoon salt, or more to taste

Tagine sauce

2 tablespoons olive oil

2 large onions, sliced

½ cup vegetable stock

1 teaspoon paprika

1 teaspoon ground cumin

½ teaspoon ground cinnamon

½ teaspoon ground turmeric

½ teaspoon salt, or more to taste

4 eggs

* Place the chunks of meat in a large bowl with the remaining kebab ingredients. Using your hands, gently massage the meat with the onions and herbs so that the juices of the onions are well incorporated with the meat. Cover with plastic wrap and leave to marinate in the fridge for 2–8 hours.

* For the sauce, heat the olive oil in a large saucepan over medium heat. Add the onions, cover the pan and leave to cook for about 10 minutes until they are soft and translucent, stirring occasionally. Uncover the pan and cook the onions for a further 15 minutes, stirring occasionally, until they turn lightly golden.

* Add the stock, paprika, cumin, cinnamon, turmeric and salt and bring to a boil over high heat. Cover the pan, reduce the heat to medium-low and simmer gently for 15 minutes to allow the spices to release their essences. If it looks like there isn't enough liquid in the pan at any point during the cooking process, add a couple tablespoons of water.

* Uncover the pan, add the chunks of marinated beef and stir to combine. Cook for about 2 minutes until the meat is no longer pink. Make some space for the eggs, then gently break them straight into the sauce, re-cover the pan and cook for 5 minutes or until the whites are set but the yolks are still runny. Serve immediately with crusty bread.

Mrouzia lamb shanks

Mrouzia is a tagine of lamb simmered in a scrumptious syrupy sauce made from onions, ras el hanout, honey and raisins until the meat is fork tender. This is such a long-standing classic that the old recipes for *mrouzia* I came across during my research all called for impressively large amounts of animal fat and honey in order to preserve the meat before the invention of modern refrigeration! This centuries-old tagine is steeped in Moroccan culture and is usually served to celebrate Eid el Kabir or special occasions. Enjoy with fluffy couscous or plenty of crusty bread.

3 tablespoons olive oil
2 lb 10 oz lamb shanks trimmed of excess fat (about 4 small or 3 large shanks)
2 large onions (14 oz), grated
4 garlic cloves, peeled and crushed
2 teaspoons ras el hanout (*see page 9* for homemade)
¼ teaspoon ground cinnamon

¾ teaspoon salt, or more to taste
generous pinch of saffron threads
1 cup vegetable stock
½ cup blanched almonds
1 cup raisins
⅓ cup clear honey
couscous or crusty bread, to serve

* Heat 2 tablespoons of the olive oil in a large saucepan over medium high-heat. Add the lamb shanks and cook until browned on each side. Make sure that the oil is very hot before adding the meat — you should hear a sizzle when the meat touches the pan, otherwise it isn't hot enough. The meat will be released naturally from the pan once browned on one side, so don't be tempted to turn it beforehand. Transfer the browned lamb shanks to a dish and set aside until ready to use.

* Reduce the heat under the saucepan to medium, add the remaining tablespoon of olive oil, the onions, garlic, ras el hanout, cinnamon, salt and saffron and cook for about 5 minutes, stirring occasionally. Return the lamb shanks to the pan, pour in the stock and bring to a boil over high heat. Cover the pan, reduce the heat to medium-low and leave to simmer gently for about 1¾ hours, stirring occasionally, until the meat is fully cooked and fork tender. If it looks like there isn't enough liquid in the pan and the tagine is drying

out at any point during the cooking process, add a couple tablespoons of water.

* Meanwhile, preheat the oven to 400°F (200°C). Spread the almonds out on a cookie sheet and roast for 10–12 minutes or until lightly golden, giving them a good stir halfway through to make sure that they roast evenly. Remove from the oven and leave until cool enough to handle, then grind using a food processor or crush with a rolling pin until coarsely ground. Set aside until ready to serve.

* Once the lamb shanks are fully cooked, remove them from the pan and set aside. Add the raisins and honey to the sauce and gently stir to combine. Cook, uncovered, over medium-low heat for about 35 minutes, stirring occasionally, until the sauce has reduced to a syrup-like consistency and the raisins are plump.

* When the sauce is ready, return the lamb shanks to the pan to warm them up and mix them with the sauce. Garnish with almonds and serve immediately with fluffy couscous or crusty bread.

Orange zest & turmeric lamb chops

I love lamb chops. No offence to my vegetarian friends, but I think there is something extremely satisfying about holding a lamb chop with your fingers and biting into it until there is nothing left but a lonely bone. My brothers and I used to have contests to see how fast we could eat a lamb chop; I lost every single time. Another reason I love lamb chops is because of how easy they are to prepare — just mix them with your favorite marinade and *voilà*! This marinade tastes like magic, with the orange and turmeric making a glowing combination that will take your taste buds on a colorful and flavorful adventure.

5 tablespoons olive oil
3 garlic cloves, peeled and crushed
finely grated zest of 2 oranges
2 tablespoons clear honey
1 tablespoon dried mint
1½ teaspoons ground turmeric
¾ teaspoon salt
1 lb 2 oz lamb chops (about 4–6)
1 large onion (7 oz), finely sliced

* Mix the olive oil, garlic, orange zest, honey, dried mint, turmeric and salt together in a small bowl.

* Lay the lamb chops in a flat dish and pour over the marinade to cover. Cover the dish with plastic wrap and leave the lamb to marinate in the fridge for 2 hours or overnight.

* Preheat the oven to 400°F (200°C). Spread the onion slices out in a roasting pan and place the lamb chops on top. Roast for 15–20 minutes according to how you like your lamb cooked. Serve immediately.

Merguez burger
with preserved lemon guacamole

Merguez is a kind of spicy sausage found everywhere across North Africa and beyond. I've always struggled to find top-quality merguez outside of my parents' home; a good merguez has the potential to give you a new passion for sausages, so just imagine what a merguez burger can do for you! For extra spiciness, I recommend adding a dash of harissa to your mayonnaise.

Merguez burger

2 tablespoons fennel seeds
2 tablespoons cumin seeds
2 tablespoons coriander seeds
½ lb ground lamb, 20% fat
½ lb ground beef, 20% fat
4 garlic cloves, peeled and crushed
⅓ cup fresh cilantro, finely chopped
2 tablespoons paprika
1 tablespoon superfine sugar
1 tablespoon dried mint
1 teaspoon salt, or more to taste
½ teaspoon cayenne pepper
½ teaspoon ground black pepper

Preserved lemon guacamole

2 ripe avocados
1 tomato, deseeded and chopped
1 shallot, finely chopped
2 small preserved lemons (2 oz; *see* page 9 for homemade), flesh and rind finely chopped
2 tablespoons finely chopped fresh cilantro
½ tablespoon lemon juice, or more to taste
½ teaspoon salt, or more to taste

To assemble

4 burger buns
mayonnaise
tomato slices
lettuce leaves

* Toast the fennel, cumin and coriander seeds in a dry skillet over medium heat for about 3 minutes until fragrant. Transfer the toasted spices to a pestle and mortar, spice or coffee grinder to roughly grind them.

* Place all the ingredients for the merguez mince in a large bowl with the ground spices and use your hands to mix them together. Cover the bowl with plastic wrap and place in the fridge until ready to use.

* Prepare the preserved lemon guacamole a few minutes before grilling the burgers (if need be, you can make it in advance and keep it, covered with plastic wrap, in the fridge, but it will lose its bright green color and turn brownish). Cut the avocados in half lengthways, remove the pits and use a large spoon to scoop out the avocado flesh into a bowl.

* Mash the avocado flesh with a fork, then add the remaining guacamole ingredients and stir together until well combined. Taste and adjust the seasoning, adding more salt and lemon juice if necessary.

* Divide the merguez burger mixture into quarters and form each quarter into a ball. Using your hands, flatten each ball into a disc ¾ inch thick. Preheat a skillet or griddle or a barbecue to medium-high heat and cook the burgers for 3–4 minutes on each side according to your liking.

* Immediately assemble your burgers by placing each merguez patty in a split burger bun with some mayonnaise, tomato slices, lettuce leaves and a serving of the preserved lemon guacamole.

Sticky ras el hanout & peach beef short ribs

"The closer to the bone, the sweeter the meat," so the old proverb goes, but if you've ever wondered whether this is true, it's time you made your own beef short ribs! I used to be very intimidated by the thought of cooking short ribs myself and would only enjoy them in restaurants — until the day I decided to woman up and started experimenting. It turns out that preparing short ribs is one of the easiest things to do at home because it's your oven that actually does all the work. Simply whip up the marinade for the ribs, transfer them to the oven, sit back and relax. Serve with sautéed greens or a velvety mashed potato.

1 lb 12 oz ripe peaches (about 4), skinned, stoned and roughly chopped
⅓ cup vegetable stock
½ cup soft light brown sugar
2½ tablespoons ras el hanout (*see* page 9 for homemade)
6 garlic cloves, peeled and crushed
3 tablespoons white wine vinegar
4 tablespoons tomato ketchup
1 teaspoon salt
½ teaspoon ground black pepper
3 lb 8 oz beef short ribs, cut into 2½ inch lengths
½ cup clear honey
1 green onion, finely sliced, to garnish

* Preheat the oven to 350°F (180°C).

* Place the peaches, stock, sugar, ras el hanout, garlic, vinegar, ketchup, salt and pepper in a food processor and process for 1 minute until smooth.

* Place the ribs, meat-side down, in a roasting pan and pour over half the marinade, making sure that all the surfaces of the ribs are coated. Tightly cover with foil and roast for about 3 hours or until the ribs are cooked through and fork tender, starting to check if they are done after 2½ hours.

* About 25 minutes before the ribs are cooked through, transfer the remaining marinade to a small saucepan and stir in the honey. Bring to a boil over high heat, then reduce the heat to medium-low and simmer for about 25 minutes until the sauce is thick and sticky, stirring occasionally.

* Remove the pan from the oven and carefully transfer the ribs to another roasting pan. Cover the ribs with the sticky sauce and roast, uncovered, for a further 10–15 minutes or until they are golden brown.

* Garnish the ribs with the green onion and serve immediately.

Kefta & olive toast

Across the Middle East and North Africa, *kefta* refers to a kind of ground meat shaped into small loaves or patties, which are then chargrilled. Pronounced "kofte" in Turkey or "kafta" in Syria, every type consistently contains two main ingredients: ground meat and spices. Fiercely loved by children and grown-ups alike, *kefta* is so ingrained in Moroccan culture that it's considered a national dish. When I was pregnant with my daughter, I had serious *kefta* cravings and the best way to overcome them quickly was to make my *Kefta* & Olive Toast. It's ready in minutes and is amazingly tasty and comforting. Back then, my pregnancy brain told me to add a squirt of ketchup and a dollop of harissa to my toast, which I'm not sure I could handle today.

Kefta
½ lb ground beef, 10–20% fat
½ lb ground lamb, 10–20% fat
1 large onion (7 oz), grated
⅓ cup flat-leaf parsley, finely chopped
⅓ cup fresh cilantro, finely chopped
4 mint sprigs, leaves picked and chopped
2 teaspoons paprika
1 teaspoon ground cumin
1 teaspoon salt
½ teaspoon ground black pepper
pinch of cayenne pepper

To serve
2 tablespoons olive oil
1 quantity of Kefta (*see left*)
4 slices of bread, chargrilled or toasted
1 cup drained pitted green olives, chopped
chopped parsley, to garnish

To make the Kefta
* Place all the ingredients in a large bowl, then use your hands or a large spoon to mix them together. Cover the bowl with plastic wrap and keep in the fridge until ready to use. Shape and cook as desired, or follow the next step.

To serve
* Heat the olive oil in a large skillet over medium-high heat. Add the *kefta* and cook, breaking up the meat with a wooden spoon, for about 5 minutes until it is no longer pink.

* Spoon the cooked *kefta* over each slice of warm chargrilled or toasted bread and top with chopped olives and chopped parsley to garnish. Serve immediately.

Kefta & lentil shakshuka

The Moroccan version of *shakshuka* is a bit different from the Levantine one, and by different I mean better! Ours contains meatballs and its tomato sauce is more aromatic and spicier. Often simply called *kefta* and egg tagine (you will never hear the word *shakshuka* in Morocco), Moroccans love this iconic dish, and what's not to love about it? Spiced *kefta* meatballs and soft poached eggs cooked in a velvety fragrant tomato sauce make the ideal combination for gustatory success. The lentils give a delicate and creamy consistency to the sauce that I love mopping up with plenty of bread.

1 recipe quantity of Kefta (*see page* 101)
2 tablespoons olive oil
14 oz can chopped tomatoes
3 garlic cloves, peeled and crushed
1 tablespoon chopped flat-leaf parsley
1 teaspoon ground cumin
1 teaspoon paprika

½ teaspoon salt
½ teaspoon superfine sugar
¼ teaspoon ground black pepper
⅔ cup canned green lentils, rinsed and drained
4 eggs
chopped fresh cilantro, to garnish
bread, to serve

* Shape the *kefta* mixture into large meatballs 1 inch in diameter, then cover with plastic wrap and keep in the fridge until ready to use.

* Place a large skillet over high heat and stir in the olive oil, tomatoes, garlic, parsley, cumin, paprika, salt, sugar and pepper. Bring to a boil, then cover the pan, reduce the heat to low and leave to simmer gently, stirring every now and then, for about 25 minutes until the mixture becomes a thick sauce. If it looks like the sauce is too dry at any point during the cooking process, add a couple tablespoons of water.

* Stir the lentils into the sauce, re-cover the pan and simmer for 5 minutes. Add the meatballs to the sauce, re-cover the pan again and cook for about 7 minutes or until they start turning brown and are just cooked through.

* Move the meatballs around to make some space for the eggs, then gently break them straight into the sauce, re-cover the pan and cook for 5 minutes or until the whites are set but the yolks are still runny. Garnish with chopped cilantro and serve immediately with bread.

Berber meat turnovers with goat cheese & harissa sauce

Ground meat cooked with sweet peppers and spices and then tucked up in puff pastry packages is an irresistible treat. I love making mini versions of these luscious pastries for dinner parties, and they're always the first to disappear — so easy to prepare yet they never fail to make a great impression. Don't forget to drizzle your baked turnovers with the goat cheese and harissa sauce to attain total gourmet satisfaction.

2 tablespoons olive oil
2 large onions, chopped
1 large red bell pepper (5 oz), cored, deseeded and chopped into ⅓ inch pieces
1 large green bell pepper (5 oz), cored, deseeded and chopped into ⅓ inch pieces
3 tablespoons finely chopped flat-leaf parsley
2 teaspoons ground paprika
1½ teaspoons ground cumin
¾ teaspoon salt, or more to taste
generous pinch of cayenne pepper, or more to taste

⅓ lb ground minced beef or lamb
½ tablespoon cornstarch
2 x 11 oz ready-rolled puff pastry sheets
1 egg, beaten
green salad, to serve

Goat cheese & harissa sauce
¼ cup soft goat cheese
3 tablespoons milk (any type)
1 tablespoon harissa, any type (see page 13 for homemade)

* Heat the olive oil in a large saucepan over medium heat. Add the onions, cover the pan and leave to cook for 10 minutes until they are soft and translucent, stirring occasionally. Uncover and cook for a further 15 minutes or until they turn lightly golden, stirring occasionally.

* Add the peppers, parsley, paprika, cumin, salt and cayenne pepper, re-cover the pan and cook for about 10 minutes until the peppers are soft, stirring occasionally.

* Increase the heat to medium, add the ground meat and cook, breaking the meat up with a wooden spoon, for about 5 minutes until it is no longer pink and all the liquid has evaporated. Stir in the cornstarch and cook for 3 minutes until the mixture thickens. Remove pan from the heat, taste and adjust the seasoning, adding more salt if necessary, then leave the filling to cool to room temperature, when you can start assembling the turnovers. Alternatively, transfer the filling to a

bowl, cover with plastic wrap and refrigerate until ready to use; it will keep for up to 2 days.

* Preheat the oven to 430°F (220°C). Line a cookie sheet with parchment paper.

* Unroll your pastry sheets onto a work surface and cut each sheet into eighths. Spoon about 4 tablespoons of the filling in the center of each rectangle. Fold one corner over the filling to meet the opposite corner to form a triangle, then seal the edges by pressing down with the tines of a fork.

* Place the turnovers on the lined cookie sheet, leaving about ¾ inch between them. Brush their tops with the beaten egg and bake for about 20 minutes until golden brown.

* Meanwhile, make the sauce. Use a fork to mix the goat cheese, milk and harissa together in a bowl, then place in the fridge until ready to serve.

* Serve the turnovers alongside the sauce and a green salad.

4
POULTRY

Couscous tfaya — Fes couscous

This couscous is very special to me, and it used to be my favorite couscous when I was a child. Both my parents are from Fes, where *tfaya* originates and I spent the majority of my childhood holidays there with my mom, grandmother and aunts, wandering around the souk of the old medina or watching them cook gigantic feasts. The whole recipe is really easy to prepare and doesn't require more than an hour's cooking on the stovetop.

3 tablespoons olive oil
2 large onions, sliced
4 garlic cloves, peeled and crushed
2 teaspoons ground turmeric
2 teaspoons ground ginger
¾ teaspoon salt, or more to taste
¼ teaspoon ground black pepper
pinch of saffron threads
6 large chicken legs
1⅔ cups chicken stock
14 oz can chickpeas, rinsed and drained
⅔ cup toasted flaked almonds, to garnish (optional)

2⅓ cups couscous, cooked according to the packet instructions and seasoned with a bit of salt and olive oil

Tfaya sauce
2 tablespoons olive oil
4 large onions, sliced
2 cups raisins
3 tablespoons clear honey
1 teaspoon ground cinnamon
½ teaspoon salt, or more to taste
½ cup chicken stock

* Heat the olive oil in a large saucepan over medium heat. Add the onions, garlic, turmeric, ginger, salt, pepper and saffron and cook for 3 minutes, stirring occasionally.

* Add the chicken legs to the pan and cook for 5 minutes, turning occasionally. Pour in the stock and bring to a boil over high heat. Cover the pan, reduce the heat to medium-low and leave to simmer gently for 45 minutes. Stir in the chickpeas, re-cover the pan and continue simmering for a further 15 minutes or until the chicken is cooked through.

* While the chicken is cooking, prepare the *tfaya* sauce. Heat the olive oil in a separate large saucepan over medium-low heat. Add the onions, cover the pan and leave to cook for about 20 minutes until they are soft and translucent, stirring occasionally. Meanwhile, soak the raisins in hot water for 10 minutes until softened, then drain and set aside.

* When the onions are soft, add the softened raisins, honey, cinnamon and salt and cook, uncovered, for about 10 minutes until the onions are lightly golden, stirring occasionally. Pour in the stock and bring to a boil over high heat, then reduce the heat to medium-low and simmer for about 25 minutes until most of the liquid has evaporated and you have a thick golden brown sauce. Taste and adjust the seasoning, adding more salt if necessary.

* By the time your *tfaya* sauce is ready, the chicken should be fully cooked and ready to be served. Taste the broth and adjust the seasoning, adding more salt if necessary. To serve, place the warm cooked couscous on a large serving plate, top with the chicken, broth and chickpeas and finally add the *tfaya* sauce. Garnish with toasted flaked almonds if desired.

Chicken kamama — Shallot & tomato chicken tagine

This tagine is a Marrakchi speciality. When I was a child, my uncle's wife, Nadia, who grew up in Marrakech, used to cook *kamama* every time our family came to visit from Brussels and I would always get excited about the mountain of shallots this tagine contains. *Kamama* is such a treat for the senses that it's a shame it isn't popular in the rest of the world. It's so incredibly decadent and Moorish, which is why I always prepare it for big celebrations. The traditional recipe calls for thick sliced onions instead of whole shallots but, like my aunt Nadia, I prefer to use shallots for their deeper, sweeter taste.

3 tablespoons olive oil
1 large onion, grated
4 garlic cloves, peeled and crushed
1 teaspoon ground turmeric
1 teaspoon ground ginger
1 teaspoon ground cinnamon
¾ teaspoon salt, or more to taste

¼ teaspoon ground black pepper
4 chicken legs
⅔ cup chicken stock
2 lb 11 oz shallots, peeled but left whole
5 tomatoes, skinned, deseeded and quartered
3 tablespoons clear honey
1 tablespoon sesame seeds, to garnish
couscous or bread, to serve

* Heat the olive oil in a large saucepan over medium heat. Add the onion, garlic, turmeric, ginger, cinnamon, salt and pepper and cook for 3 minutes, stirring occasionally.

* Add the chicken legs to the pan and cook for 5 minutes, turning the chicken occasionally. Pour in the stock and bring to a boil over high heat. Cover the pan, reduce the heat to medium-low and leave to simmer gently for 25 minutes.

* Preheat the oven to 400°F (200°C). Remove the chicken legs from the pan and place them, skin-side up, in a deep roasting pan, then immediately transfer to the oven. Meanwhile, add the shallots and tomatoes to the saucepan along with the honey and mix them with the stock and the onion. Bring to a boil over high heat, then cover the pan, reduce the heat to medium-low and leave to simmer gently for about 20 minutes

until the shallots are soft.

* Taste the sauce and adjust the seasoning, adding more salt if necessary. Remove the roasting pan from the oven and carefully pour the contents of the saucepan around the chicken legs. Return the pan to the oven and roast the chicken for a further 25 minutes or until the chicken is cooked through and the shallots are golden. Garnish with the sesame seeds and serve immediately with warm couscous or bread.

Chorba beida — White chicken soup

In Morocco and all over North Africa, there are countless types of *chorba*, but all of them
are based on the same principle: a clear soup made from meat or poultry and pulses.
While researching different kinds of *chorba* in Morocco, I came across *chorba beida*,
which translates from Arabic to "white soup" and originated from Algiers.
The interesting combination of egg yolk and lemon juice beautifully highlights the few
simple ingredients and spices used in this soup, and gives it its soft and tangy taste as well
as its whitish color. *Chorba beida* is without a doubt my favorite *chorba*.

————

1 tablespoon unsalted butter
1 tablespoon olive oil
2 large onions, chopped
10.5 oz boneless, skinless chicken thighs or breasts,
chopped into chunks
¾ teaspoon salt, or more to taste
½ teaspoon ground black pepper
¼ teaspoon ground cinnamon
2 cups chicken stock

3 cups water
3.5 oz dried spaghetti, broken into 1 inch lengths
5 oz (drained weight) canned chickpeas,
rinsed and drained
3 tablespoons lemon juice
⅓ cup flat-leaf parsley, finely chopped,
plus extra to serve
1 egg yolk

————

* Melt the butter with the olive oil in a large
saucepan over medium heat. Add the onions,
cover the pan and cook for about 10 minutes until
they are soft and translucent, stirring occasionally.
Add the chicken, salt, pepper and cinnamon, stir
to combine and cook, uncovered, stirring
occasionally, for about 5 minutes.

* Pour in the stock and measured water and bring
to a boil over high heat. Re-cover the pan, reduce
the heat to medium-low and leave to simmer
gently for 30 minutes. By then, the chicken pieces
should be fully cooked, but if not, leave to simmer
for a few more minutes.

* Throw in the broken spaghetti and chickpeas and
bring to a boil over high heat, then reduce the heat
to medium-low and leave to simmer, uncovered,
according to the packet instructions until the
spaghetti is cooked.

* Meanwhile, place the lemon juice, parsley and egg
yolk in a small bowl and mix together with a fork.

* Once the spaghetti is cooked, pour the egg yolk
mixture into the pan and stir with a wooden
spoon to combine. Taste and adjust the seasoning,
adding salt if necessary. Leave to simmer for
about 2 minutes, then remove the pan from the
heat and serve immediately with extra chopped
parsley.

Chicken, carrot & charred lemon tagine

Tagine dial djaj wa khizo is what Moroccans call this special seasonal tagine that they prepare as soon as carrot season begins. It's beautifully aromatic and tangy and is one of the most family- and child-friendly meals anyone can serve. Who doesn't like a good chicken tagine and who doesn't like carrots, right? If you are feeling lazy, omit the burned lemons, but I find that they give the tagine more depth and I can't resist their charred appearance.

4 tablespoons olive oil, plus extra for
rubbing the lemons and to serve
4 large chicken legs
1 large onion, grated
4 garlic cloves, peeled and crushed
1 teaspoon ground turmeric
1 teaspoon ground ginger

¾ teaspoon salt, or more to taste
¼ teaspoon ground black pepper
¾ cup vegetable stock
1 lb 5 oz carrots, peeled and cut into ½ inch cubes
3 lemons
couscous or bread, to serve

* Heat 2 tablespoons of the olive oil in a large saucepan over medium-high heat. Add the chicken legs (in batches if necessary), skin-side down, and sear for about 5 minutes until golden brown. Make sure that the oil is very hot before adding the chicken — you should hear a sizzle when the skin touches the pan, otherwise it isn't hot enough. The skin will be released naturally from the chicken flesh once seared, so don't be tempted to remove it beforehand. Transfer the seared chicken to a dish and set aside until you are ready to use it.

* Reduce the heat under the saucepan to medium and heat the remaining 2 tablespoons olive oil. Add the onion, garlic, turmeric, ginger, salt and pepper and cook for 5 minutes, stirring occasionally. Return all the chicken legs to the pan and pour in the stock. Bring to a boil over high heat, then reduce the heat to medium-low, cover the pan and leave to simmer gently for 45 minutes or until the chicken is almost cooked, stirring occasionally. If it looks like there isn't enough liquid in the pan at any point

during the cooking process, add a couple tablespoons of water.

* Remove the chicken briefly from the pan while you throw in the carrots, then return the chicken legs to the pan, laying them on top of the carrots. Re-cover the pan — this will help the carrots to cook faster — then cook for about 15 minutes or until the carrots and the chicken are both cooked through.

* Meanwhile, burn the lemons. Heat a small, dry skillet over medium-high heat. Cut the lemons in half and use your fingers to rub their flesh with a bit of olive oil. Place the lemons, cut-side down, in the pan and cook for about 3 minutes or until their flesh is charred.

* When the chicken and carrots are cooked, taste the broth and adjust the seasoning, adding more salt if necessary. Squeeze 2 burned lemon halves over the dish and generously drizzle with olive oil. Serve immediately with the remaining burned lemons on the side, along with some warm couscous or bread.

Chicken brania — Broken eggplant & chickpea chicken tagine

Brania is a tagine that originates from Tlemcen, a city in northwestern Algeria, not far from the Moroccan border. Since its exportation to Morocco, *brania* has experienced many alterations, but there's one thing that never changes about this tagine: it's always topped with eggplant. Sometimes the eggplant is deep-fried, while other times it's broken into pieces, depending I guess on the family and the region. Luckily, my uncle Anouar's wife is an Algerian from Tlemcen, and she kindly gave me her mother's recipe for an authentic lip-smacking *brania*, which I am delighted to share with you (*see* photograph on pages 116-117).

4 tablespoons olive oil
4 chicken legs
2 large onions, sliced
5 garlic cloves, peeled and crushed
1½ teaspoons caraway seeds
1 teaspoon paprika
1 teaspoon ground cumin
¾ teaspoon salt, or more to taste
½ teaspoon ground coriander
¼ teaspoon ground black pepper
¾ cup chicken stock
14 oz can chickpeas, rinsed and drained
cilantro leaves, to garnish

Broken eggplant
4 tablespoons olive oil
3 large eggplant, peeled and chopped into large chunks
2 garlic cloves, peeled and crushed
½ teaspoon salt, or more to taste

* Heat 2 tablespoons of the olive oil in a large saucepan over medium-high heat. Add the chicken legs (in batches if necessary), skin-side down, and sear for about 5 minutes until golden brown. Make sure that the oil is very hot before adding the chicken — you should hear a sizzle when the skin touches the pan, otherwise it isn't hot enough. The skin will be released naturally from the chicken flesh once seared, so don't be tempted to remove it beforehand. Transfer the seared chicken to a dish and set aside until ready to use.

* Reduce the heat under the saucepan to medium-low and heat the remaining 2 tablespoons olive oil. Add the onions, cover the pan and leave to cook for about 10 minutes or until they are soft and translucent, stirring occasionally. Add the garlic, caraway seeds, paprika, cumin, salt, ground coriander and pepper and cook for 5 minutes, stirring occasionally. Return all the chicken legs to the pan and pour in the stock. Bring to a boil over high heat, then re-cover the pan, reduce the heat to medium-low and leave to simmer gently

for 45 minutes. Stir in the chickpeas, re-cover the pan again and simmer for a further 15 minutes or until the chicken is cooked through.

* While the chicken is cooking, prepare the broken eggplant. Heat the olive oil in a large skillet. Add the eggplant, garlic and salt, cover the pan and leave to cook gently over medium-low heat for about 30 minutes until the eggplant are soft, stirring occasionally to make sure that the eggplant don't stick to the base of the pan.

* Uncover the skillet and, using the back of a wooden spoon, break the eggplant into pieces. Increase the heat to medium and cook for about 5 minutes or until all the liquid has evaporated, stirring occasionally. Taste the eggplant and season with more salt as necessary. Remove the pan from the heat and set aside until ready to serve.

* Taste the chicken broth and adjust the seasoning, adding more salt if necessary. Transfer the chicken and chickpeas to a large serving plate, top with the broken eggplant, garnish with cilantro leaves and serve immediately.

Chicken mchermel — Preserved lemon, olive & chicken tagine

I kept going back and forth over whether or not I should include this recipe in my book. While this is without a doubt one of the most famous Moroccan tagines, I wasn't sure that the world needed another version of it. But I changed my mind because my chicken *mchermel* really is like no other. It has all the irresistible Moroccan-scented, lemony flavors, plus the perfect sauce-to-onion ratio, which is what makes all the difference.

4 tablespoons olive oil
4 chicken legs
4 large onions, sliced
½ cup fresh cilantro, chopped
4 garlic cloves, peeled and crushed
1 teaspoon paprika
1 teaspoon ground cumin
¾ teaspoon salt, or more to taste
¼ teaspoon ground black pepper

pinch of saffron threads
⅔ cup chicken stock
3 tablespoons lemon juice
4 small preserved lemons (4 oz; *see* page 9 for homemade), flesh and rind finely chopped, plus extra to serve
1 cup red-brown olives, such as Kalamata, plus extra to serve
crusty bread or couscous, to serve

* Heat 2 tablespoons of the olive oil in a large saucepan over medium-high heat. Add the chicken legs (in batches if necessary), skin-side down, and sear for about 5 minutes until golden brown. Make sure that the oil is very hot before adding the chicken — you should hear a sizzle when the skin touches the pan, otherwise it isn't hot enough. The skin will be released naturally from the chicken flesh once seared, so don't be tempted to remove it beforehand. Transfer the seared chicken to a dish and set aside until ready to use.

* Reduce the heat under the saucepan to medium-low and heat the remaining 2 tablespoons olive oil. Add the onions, cover the pan and leave to cook for about 20 minutes or until they are soft and translucent, stirring occasionally.

* Add the cilantro, garlic, paprika, cumin, salt, pepper and saffron to the pan and cook, uncovered and stirring occasionally, for 5

minutes. Return the chicken legs to the pan, pour in the stock and lemon juice and bring to a boil over high heat. Re-cover the pan, reduce the heat to medium-low and leave to simmer gently for about 1 hour or until the chicken is fully cooked.

* Remove the chicken legs from the pan and set aside. Continue cooking the onion sauce over medium-low heat, uncovered and stirring occasionally, for about 30 minutes or until most of the liquid has evaporated.

* Stir the chopped preserved lemons and the olives into the reduced sauce and cook for a further 10 minutes. Taste and adjust the seasoning, adding more salt if necessary.

* To serve, return the chicken legs to the pan for about 5 minutes to warm them through in the sauce. Scatter with extra chopped preserved lemon and olives and serve immediately with crusty bread or warm couscous.

Chicken kdra with apricots

Kdra refers to a specific kind of tagine where pieces of meat or poultry are cooked slowly with turmeric, ground ginger, chickpeas and sometimes blanched almonds. Throw in some apricots for sweetness and you've got yourself a knockout tagine for you and your guests to consume without moderation.

4 tablespoons olive oil
4 large chicken legs
3 large onions, sliced
4 garlic cloves, peeled and crushed
1 teaspoon ground turmeric
1 teaspoon ground ginger
¾ teaspoon salt, or more to taste
¼ teaspoon ground black pepper

⅔ cup vegetable stock
1 small bunch of fresh cilantro, tied together with kitchen string
14 oz can chickpeas, rinsed and drained
⅔ cup dried apricots
¾ cup blanched almonds
roughly chopped flat-leaf parsley, to garnish
crusty bread or couscous, to serve

* Heat 2 tablespoons of the olive oil in a large saucepan over medium-high heat. Add the chicken legs (in batches if necessary), skin-side down, and sear for about 5 minutes until golden brown. Make sure that the oil is very hot before adding the chicken — you should hear a sizzle when the skin touches the pan, otherwise it isn't hot enough. The skin will be released naturally from the chicken flesh once seared, so don't be tempted to remove it beforehand. Transfer the seared chicken to a dish and set aside until ready to use.

* Reduce the heat under the saucepan to medium-low and heat the remaining 2 tablespoons olive oil. Add the onions, cover the pan and leave to cook for about 15 minutes or until they are soft and translucent, stirring occasionally. Add the garlic, turmeric, ginger, salt and pepper and cook for 5 minutes, stirring occasionally. Return the chicken legs to the pan, pour in the stock and add the cilantro bouquet. Bring to a boil over high heat, then cover the pan, reduce the heat to medium-low and leave to simmer gently for 30 minutes.

* Remove and discard the cilantro bouquet, then stir in the chickpeas, apricots and almonds and give the contents of the pan a good stir. Bring back to a boil over high heat, then re-cover the pan, reduce the heat to medium-low and leave to simmer for a further 30 minutes or until the chicken is fully cooked. If it looks like there isn't enough liquid in the pan at any point during the cooking process, add a couple tablespoons of water.

* Garnish with chopped parsley and serve immediately with crusty bread or warm couscous.

Spicy chicken livers

Liver is a tricky thing to serve, as people either love it or hate it. If you don't like it, that's absolutely fine and you may just want to move on to the next page. But if you do like it, stick around because I've got one gloriously tasty recipe for you. This dish is usually made with veal liver instead of chicken livers, but I prefer the latter for its profound poultry flavor and creamy texture — plus, it has great nutritional value. Serve with extra cayenne pepper on the side so that your guests can customize their serving according to how hot they like it.

1 tablespoon olive oil
1 large onion, chopped
3 tablespoons all-purpose flour
3 tablespoons water
14 oz chicken livers, washed and cut into 1 inch chunks
1 green onion, finely sliced, to garnish

¾ cup fresh cilantro, finely chopped
2 tablespoons lemon juice
2 teaspoons paprika
1 teaspoon ground cumin
1 teaspoon salt
¼ heaped teaspoon cayenne pepper, or more to taste, plus extra to serve

Marinade
3 tablespoons olive oil
4 garlic cloves, peeled and crushed

To serve
lemon wedges
bread

* Heat the olive oil in a large skillet over medium heat. Add the onion, cover the pan and leave to cook for about 10 minutes, stirring occasionally, until soft and translucent.

* Meanwhile, stir all the ingredients for the marinade together in a small bowl until smooth.

* Add the marinade, flour and water to the skillet and cook, stirring, until the mixture has thickened. Then add the livers, re-cover the pan and cook for about 15 minutes or until they are cooked through — you will know when they are done when they turn brown and feel firm.

* Garnish with green onion and serve immediately with lemon wedges and cayenne pepper on the side, along with some bread.

Buttermilk chicken kebabs

I am bending the rules of this recipe slightly, but it's definitely in a good cause: I have added buttermilk to the traditional marinade for the chicken to give a bright, tangy flavor to the kebabs — this also help soften the chicken. Buttermilk is not commonly used to marinate chicken or meat in Morocco, but it's a great tenderizer, and I never miss an opportunity to add it to my favorite classics such as my Cumin & Buttermilk Cornbread (*see* page 185). I love the smokiness that the barbecue gives to kebabs in general, but these kebabs are so beautifully tasty that they can be cooked in a skillet and still come out spectacularly.

⅓ cup buttermilk
½ cup fresh cilantro, finely chopped
3 garlic cloves, peeled and chopped
2 tablespoons lemon juice
2 tablespoons olive oil
1 tablespoon clear honey
1 teaspoon ground turmeric
1 teaspoon ground ginger
1 teaspoon ground cumin
½ teaspoon salt, or more to taste
½ teaspoon ground black pepper
1 lb 2 oz boneless, skinless chicken thighs or
breasts, cut into bite-sized chunks

* Place all the ingredients, except the chicken, in a large bowl and stir to combine. Add the chicken and turn to coat with the marinade. Cover with plastic wrap and leave to marinate in the fridge for 2–12 hours.

* When ready to serve, thread the pieces of chicken on to skewers. Preheat a barbecue or heat a griddle or skillet over high heat. Place the skewers on your barbecue or skillet and cook for 5 minutes on each side, turning every now and then, until golden on all sides and cooked through. Serve immediately.

Duck & cannellini bean casserole with caraway & dried figs

Caraway and dried figs are widely used in tagines and other Moroccan dishes, and I absolutely love the association of these two ingredients, so I had to include something "caraway and dried figs" in this book. Before I went to cookery school, I was under the impression that duck was a very particular sort of poultry and therefore cooking it seemed intimidating. The truth is, you can cook duck pretty much the same way you cook chicken. This combination of a roasted duck and an intensely flavored casserole is extremely hard to resist, and have I mentioned that this meal is ready in an hour?

4 duck legs
2 tablespoons unsalted butter
7 oz shallots, chopped
5.5 oz carrots, peeled and chopped
5 oz celery, chopped
1 cup dried figs, roughly chopped
3 garlic cloves, peeled and chopped

1½ teaspoons caraway seeds
½ teaspoon dried thyme
¼ teaspoon ground black pepper
⅔ cup vegetable stock
14 oz can cannellini beans, rinsed and drained
salt
roughly chopped flat-leaf parsley, to garnish

* Preheat the oven to 375°F (190°C).

* Pat the duck legs dry with paper towel and prick the skin all over with a fork. Rub ½ teaspoon salt into the duck leg skin, then place the legs, skin-side up, in a roasting pan. Roast for 50 minutes–1 hour, depending on the size of the duck legs, until golden and crisp.

* Meanwhile, prepare the casserole. Melt the butter in a large saucepan over medium heat. Add the shallots, cover the pan and cook for about 10 minutes, stirring occasionally, until they are soft and translucent. Add the carrots, celery, figs, garlic, caraway seeds, thyme, ½ teaspoon salt and the pepper, give the contents of the pan a good stir, then simmer, uncovered and stirring occasionally, for 5 minutes.

* Pour in the stock and bring to a boil over high heat, then re-cover the pan, reduce the heat to low and leave to simmer gently for 35 minutes. By then, the carrot and celery pieces should be fully cooked, but if not, leave to simmer for a few more minutes.

* Stir in the cannellini beans and cook, uncovered, for a further 10 minutes. Taste and adjust the seasoning, adding more salt if necessary. If it looks like there isn't enough liquid in the pan at any point during the cooking process, add a few tablespoons of water.

* At this stage, the roasted duck should be fully cooked and crisp. To serve, ladle the bean casserole into 4 shallow bowls and top each serving with a duck leg. Garnish with chopped parsley.

Harissa & lemon chicken tray bake with sweet potatoes & cauliflower

We all need recipes like this sometimes, when just thinking about what to cook and how to cook it feels like a gigantic effort; it happens to the best of us. On those occasions, a one-bowl/one-pan approach is the answer — the kind where you just throw ingredients together and *voilà*, there's a delicious meal that you can proudly take credit for. So if you are on the lookout for that type of recipe, you're on the right page, but even if not, you're still on the right page. Harissa and lemon are like bread and butter: they work so well together, we should marry them.

2 onions (14 oz), sliced
8 garlic cloves, peeled but left whole
4 large chicken legs
1 large sweet potato (½ lb), cut into large chunks
10.5 oz cauliflower florets
2 lemons, sliced

Marinade

a scant cup of vegetable stock
finely grated zest of 3 lemons
3 tablespoons lemon juice
3 garlic cloves, peeled and crushed
3 tablespoons Harissa (any type; *see page 13*), plus extra to serve
2 tablespoons olive oil
2 tablespoons finely chopped fresh cilantro
¾ teaspoon salt, or more to taste

* Preheat the oven to 400°F (200°C).

* Mix all the marinade ingredients together in a bowl.

* Spread the onions out in a deep roasting pan and scatter the garlic cloves all over. Place the chicken legs, skin-side up, on top with sweet potato chunks and cauliflower florets. Pour over the marinade and turn the chicken legs several times

to ensure that they are fully coated with the marinade. Top the whole dish with lemon slices.

* Bake for about 1 hour or until the chicken is golden and cooked through. Serve the chicken and vegetables immediately with extra harissa.

Rainbow couscous stuffed poussins

I love roasting these stuffed poussins and cutting them in half to serve — they always make a big impression. The insides look like confetti with the pistachios, cranberries, parsley and preserved lemon creating a rainbow of color that is just as tasty as it looks. I also love serving poussins in general; I find them tastier and more tender than chicken and so charmingly cute. This recipe is perfect for a casual meal because a whole stuffed poussin contains everything one needs, so you don't need to worry about sides. Feel free to swap the nuts and cranberries for any other nut or dried fruit of your choice. I usually leave the birds to marinate overnight and stuff them just before roasting.

¼ cup olive oil
1 teaspoon ground turmeric
1 teaspoon ground cumin
1 teaspoon ground coriander
1 teaspoon ground ginger
1 teaspoon salt
½ teaspoon ground black pepper
4 poussins

Stuffing

⅔ cup couscous, cooked according to the packet instructions
4 small preserved lemons (4 oz; *see* page 9), flesh and rind finely chopped
¾ cup dried cranberries
2 oz pine nuts, toasted
½ cup unsalted shelled pistachio nuts, roughly chopped
¼ cup olive oil
¾ cup flat-leaf parsley, finely chopped
2 garlic cloves, peeled and crushed
2 tablespoons red wine vinegar
½ teaspoon salt, or more to taste

* Preheat the oven to 400°F (200°C).

* Mix the olive oil, turmeric, cumin, coriander, ginger, salt and pepper together in a large bowl. Add the poussins and turn to coat with the marinade. Cover with plastic wrap and leave to marinate in the fridge for 2–12 hours.

* Mix all the ingredients for the stuffing together in a separate large bowl, then taste and adjust the seasoning, adding more salt if necessary.

* When ready to cook, place the poussins, breast-side up, in a roasting pan and stuff each with one-quarter of the couscous mixture. Make sure that the birds are tightly stuffed by packing the stuffing down firmly as you go. Secure each cavity closed with a toothpick.

* Roast the stuffed poussins for 45–50 minutes or until they are golden brown, and when you pierce the thickest part of the thigh with a knife the juices run clear. Serve immediately.

My chicken bastila

My entire family, my husband and I included, love chicken *bastila* so much that we served it as the main course at our wedding. In fact, for many Moroccans, *bastila* is the sacred symbol of a festive meal, and for a very good reason: a single bite has the ability to transport you to somewhere between the Atlas Mountains and the Sahara Desert. In my opinion, it is one of the most enchanting and delightful meals you can hope to experience. Its preparation may come across as a bit challenging, but the truth is there's nothing difficult about it — it just requires some time. Over the years, I have made a few adjustments to my mom's recipe and added pistachios and lemon zest to her classic *bastila*, and this is now my favorite way to enjoy it. If you prepare all the fillings on the same day, you can keep the assembled *bastila* in the fridge for up to two days. Alternatively, you can freeze them for up to two months. In which case, there is no need to defrost them — simply transfer the frozen *bastila* directly to the oven, but note that they will take 35–40 minutes to cook.

3 tablespoons olive oil
4 large onions, sliced
1 lb 9 oz boneless, skinless chicken thighs or breasts
½ cup fresh cilantro, finely chopped
3 garlic cloves, peeled and crushed
1 teaspoon ras el hanout (*see* page 9 for homemade)
¼ teaspoon ground turmeric
¼ teaspoon ground ginger
⅛ teaspoon ground black pepper
⅔ cup chicken stock

2 tablespoons clear honey
2 teaspoons ground cinnamon, plus extra to serve
¾ cup blanched almonds
¾ cup unsalted shelled pistachio nuts
2 tablespoons superfine sugar
3½ tablespoons unsalted butter
5 large eggs, plus 1 egg yolk
11 oz filo pastry sheets
finely grated zest of 3 lemons
confectioner's sugar, for dusting
salt

* Heat the olive oil in a large saucepan over medium heat. Add the onions, cover the pan and leave to cook for about 20 minutes until they are soft and translucent, stirring occasionally. Add the chicken, cilantro, garlic, ras el hanout, turmeric, ginger, ½ teaspoon salt and the pepper, stir to combine and cook, uncovered, for 5 minutes.

* Pour in the stock and bring to a boil over high heat. Cover the pan, reduce the heat to medium-low and leave to simmer gently for 50 minutes until the chicken is fully cooked, stirring occasionally but making sure that you don't break up the chicken pieces. If it looks like there isn't enough liquid in the pan at any point during the cooking process, add a few tablespoons of water. Remove the chicken from the pan and set aside to cool.

Continued on the next page...

* Once the chicken has cooled, chop it or pull it apart into ⅓ inch pieces and refrigerate until ready to use.

* Once the onions are ready, taste and adjust the seasoning, adding more salt if necessary, then transfer to a bowl and leave to cool to room temperature.

* You can start assembling the *bastila* once all the filling ingredients have cooled; warm fillings will moisten or may damage the filo pastry. Alternatively, cover the scrambled egg and onion bowls with plastic wrap and keep in the fridge along with the chicken until ready to use.

* Preheat the oven to 400°F (200°C). Line a cookie sheet with parchment paper. Melt the remaining butter in a microwave or in a small saucepan on the stovetop.

* Use a sharp knife to cut the filo pastry sheets into 12 squares of about 5 inches. Keep them covered with a dish towel to prevent them from drying out. Lay a filo square on a work surface and lightly brush it with melted butter, then top with another filo square and brush that with butter. Gently place the 2 layers of filo in the base of a small shallow ramekin or dish about 4 inches in diameter, with the excess pastry overhanging the edges.

* Add the filling ingredients to the dish in the following order: a portion of chicken chunks, a portion of caramelized onions, a portion of scrambled eggs, a portion of ground almonds and pistachios and finally the zest of half a lemon. Each portion should be enough to cover the base of the dish, bearing in my mind that you will need 6 equal-sized portions of filling for each pie.

* Fold the overhanging filo pastry over the top of the filling to cover and brush lightly with melted butter. Carefully flip the *bastila* over and remove it from the dish. Brush with the egg yolk and place on the lined cookie sheet. Repeat the same process with the remaining filo squares and fillings.

* Bake the *bastila* for about 25 minutes until golden brown. Serve immediately with a dusting of confectioner's sugar and cinnamon.

* Stir the honey and 1 teaspoon of the cinnamon into the pan and continue cooking the onions over medium-low heat, uncovered, for about 50 minutes until they are golden brown and all the liquid has evaporated. Stir occasionally to prevent the onions from sticking to the base of the pan.

* Meanwhile, prepare the rest of the filling. Preheat the oven to 400°F (200°C). Spread the almonds and pistachios out on a cookie sheet and roast for about 10–12 minutes until lightly browned, giving them a good stir halfway through to make sure that they roast evenly. Remove from the oven and leave to cool to room temperature, then grind using a food processor or crush with a rolling pin until coarsely ground. Mix with the superfine sugar and the remaining 1 teaspoon of cinnamon, then set aside until ready to use.

* Melt 1 tablespoon of the butter in a small skillet over medium heat, break the 5 whole eggs into the pan, add a pinch of salt and cook, gently stirring with a wooden spoon, for a few minutes until scrambled and fully set — make sure that your scrambled eggs aren't runny, otherwise they will adversely affect the filo pastry during the assembling process. Transfer to a bowl and leave to cool to room temperature.

Quick chicken tagine hand pies

For as long as I can remember, my mom would make our packed lunch every morning before we left for school in Brussels. Very often, yesterday's tagine leftovers would end up as a filling in a piece of crusty French baguette. Sounds amazing, right? Well, to be honest, I wasn't really excited about that because my sandwich would always smell and look weird (or that's what my classmates used to say). Why couldn't she just stuff my sandwich with cheese? Obviously, I didn't know how lucky I was back then. These hand pies (*see* photographs on pages 134-5) are like a grown-up version of those sandwiches my mom used to make for us. Quick to prepare, loaded with Moroccan flavors and easy to eat on the go, they're the perfect hand-held starter or snack.

2 tablespoons olive oil

2 large onions, finely sliced

10.5 oz boneless, skinless chicken thighs or breasts, cut into ⅓ inch chunks

4 tablespoons chicken stock

2 garlic cloves, peeled and crushed

½ teaspoon ground turmeric

½ teaspoon ground ginger

½ teaspoon salt, or more to taste

⅛ teaspoon ground black pepper

2 small preserved lemons (2 oz; *see* page 9 for homemade), flesh and rind finely chopped

½ cup drained pitted green olives, finely chopped

⅓ cup fresh cilantro, finely chopped

3 green onions, thinly sliced

2 x 11 oz ready-rolled puff pastry sheets

1 egg yolk, to glaze

harissa, any type (*see* page 13 for homemade), to serve

* Heat the olive oil in a large saucepan over medium heat. Add the onions, cover the pan and leave to cook for about 10 minutes until they are soft and translucent, stirring occasionally.

* Stir in the chicken, stock, garlic, turmeric, ginger, salt and pepper, then re-cover the pan, reduce the heat to medium-low and simmer gently for about 12 minutes until the chicken is cooked.

* Uncover the pan and cook over medium heat for about 5 minutes until all the liquid has evaporated, stirring occasionally. Transfer the chicken mixture to a large bowl, add the preserved lemons, olives, cilantro and green onions and mix together. Taste and adjust the seasoning, adding more salt if necessary. Leave the filling to cool to room temperature, when you can start assembling the pies.

* Preheat the oven to 400°F (200°C). Line a cookie sheet with parchment paper.

* Unroll the pastry sheets on to a work surface. Using a ¾ inch round dish as a guide, cut out as many circles from the pastry as possible with a sharp knife.

* Knead any leftovers of pastry back together, roll out with a rolling pin and cut out more circles — you should be able to make 12 in total.

* Place about 2 tablespoons of the chicken mixture in the center of a pastry circle. Dip your fingers in water and brush around the edge of the pastry circle, then fold it over in half, press the edges firmly together and then seal by pressing down on them with the tines of a fork. Transfer the hand pie to the lined cookie sheet. Repeat the same process with the remaining chicken mixture and pastry circles.

* Brush the pies with the egg yolk, then bake for about 25 minutes or until golden brown. Serve warm or at room temperature.

5
SEAFOOD

Fragrant seafood & tomato tagine

This tagine is seafood paradise on a plate, or at least that's how I like to think of it. I developed this recipe a few years ago when I was trying to come up with a seafood tagine to surpass all others — one that every single person would love. So this is supposedly the definitive seafood tagine recipe — charmingly fragrant, not too sweet, not too spicy and full of seafood goodness. So far it has succeeded in making everyone who has tried it happy. I love this topped with a generous sprinkling of feta, which I realize isn't a typical Moroccan ingredient, but it gives a nice salty, tangy kick to the whole dish.

3 tablespoons olive oil
2 large onions (14 oz), sliced
2 x 14 oz cans chopped tomatoes
1 green bell pepper, cored, deseeded and sliced into strips
1 red bell pepper, cored, deseeded and sliced into strips
1 carrot, peeled and sliced
3.5 oz celery, finely chopped
2 tablespoons finely chopped fresh cilantro
1 teaspoon paprika
1 teaspoon ground turmeric
1 teaspoon ground cumin
1 teaspoon ground ginger

¾ teaspoon salt, or more to taste
½ teaspoon ground cinnamon
½ teaspoon superfine sugar
¼ teaspoon ground black pepper
pinch of cayenne pepper, or more to taste
1 lb 2 oz live mussels
1 lb 2 oz cleaned squid tentacles and/or tubes sliced into rings ⅓ inch thick
10.5 oz uncooked peeled prawns

To serve
⅓ cup feta cheese, crumbled
bread or couscous

* Heat the olive oil in a large saucepan over medium-low heat. Add the onions, cover the pan and leave to cook for about 10 minutes or until they are soft and translucent, stirring occasionally. Add all the remaining ingredients, except the seafood and feta. Bring to a boil over high heat, then re-cover the pan, reduce the heat to medium-low and simmer gently for 1 hour or until you have a fragrant sauce.

* Meanwhile, prepare your mussels. Sort through them and chuck out any with damaged shells or that don't shut when lightly tapped on a surface. Pull away any beards and scrape off any barnacles attached to the shells with a knife, then rinse thoroughly under cold running water and drain.

* Taste the sauce and adjust the seasoning, adding more salt if necessary. Once the sauce is ready, it's time to cook your seafood, but make sure that you are ready to serve before adding it because it will cook within minutes. Don't forget that the sauce has to be warm in order to cook the seafood, so if you have prepared it in advance and it's cold then reheat it before adding the seafood. Throw in the prepared mussels, squid and prawns, then give everything a good stir to ensure that the seafood is well coated with the sauce. Cover the pan and cook for 5–7 minutes or until the mussel shells have opened and the other seafood is just cooked — be careful not to overcook, otherwise it will become very chewy. Discard any mussels that have failed to open.

* Sprinkle with feta and serve immediately with bread or couscous.

Classic oven-baked fish tagine

If I was ever asked to pick a seafood dish that would represent Moroccan cuisine, it would definitely be this one. This tagine is Morocco on a plate, and if you travel around the country, you will find it everywhere. Traditionally, this dish is served "family style," which means that it's prepared with a whole 6.5 lb fish instead of individual-sized fish. I have adapted this recipe to my London routine because, although I love to cook for 12 people, it doesn't happen on a regular basis. Make sure that you don't cut the potato slices too thickly here, otherwise they will take too long to cook, so if you have one, I would recommend using a mandoline.

———

3 small preserved lemons (about 3 oz; *see* page 9 for homemade)

1 recipe quantity of Chermoula (*see* page 142)

2 x 1 lb 5 oz or 4 x 10.5 oz sea bass (or any other type of white fish), cleaned and gutted

olive oil, for oiling

2 large potatoes (14 oz), peeled and thinly sliced

2 bell peppers, ideally 1 red and 1 green, cored, deseeded and sliced into rings ⅓ inch thick

2 large tomatoes, sliced

⅓ cup drained pitted green olives, roughly sliced

1 lemon, thinly sliced

crusty bread, to serve

———

* Finely chop the preserved lemons and mix with the chermoula. If necessary, add a few tablespoons of water to make it a pouring consistency. Using your hands, cover the outsides and insides of the fish with half the chermoula. Cover the fish with plastic wrap and leave to marinate in the fridge for up to 12 hours until ready to cook — the longer they marinate, the better.

* Preheat the oven to 400°F (200°C). Lightly oil a large ovenproof dish. Add the potato, pepper and tomato slices with the remaining chermoula and toss to ensure everything is coated with the chermoula. Cover the dish tightly with aluminum foil and bake for about 45 minutes until the potatoes are nearly cooked.

* Remove the dish from the oven, lift off the foil (reserve it) and arrange the fish on top of the vegetables. Top with the olives and lemon slices, then re-cover the dish tightly with the foil. Bake for a further 12–15 minutes until the potatoes and the fish are both cooked. Serve immediately with crusty bread.

Chermoula

Although chermoula is traditionally used in Moroccan cooking as a flavoring for fish and vegetables (*see* page 89), I personally love it with anything savoury. A little bit of chermoula added to your food as a dressing or a marinade will go a long way. Depending on how finely you chop your herbs, you might need to add a few splashes of water to make your chermoula spreadable. I like to use a combination of cilantro and parsley for my chermoula, but feel free to substitute one for the other if you prefer.

4 tablespoons olive oil
3 garlic cloves, peeled and finely chopped
½ cup fresh cilantro, finely chopped
½ cup flat-leaf parsley, finely chopped
2 tablespoons lemon juice
2 teaspoons paprika
1 teaspoon ground cumin
1 teaspoon salt, or more to taste
pinch of cayenne pepper

* Stir all the ingredients together in a bowl until smooth.

* Store in a clean airtight container in the fridge for up to 5 days.

Lemon, honey, rose & Swiss chard stuffed bream

I like to come up with unusual ways to stuff sea bream, and this is such an interesting combination. You might think that roses and fish wouldn't work together, but the result is quite the opposite. The fish ends up tasting extremely refreshing and lightly perfumed. It's definitely a recipe to try when you are in a rush yet have to prepare an impressive meal. I recommend serving it with couscous or roasted potatoes.

2 tablespoons olive oil, plus extra for oiling and drizzling

1 lb 5 oz Swiss chard, stalks removed, leaves cut into strips 1 inch wide

3 tablespoons clear honey

finely grated zest of 2 lemons

3 tablespoons lemon juice

2 tablespoons dried edible rose petals, plus extra for sprinkling

2 teaspoons cornstarch

3 tablespoons pine nuts

3 x 14 oz or 4 x 10.5 oz sea breams, cleaned and gutted

salt and pepper

* Heat the olive oil in a large saucepan over medium-low heat. Add the chard, then stir in the honey, lemon zest and juice, rose petals, ½ teaspoon salt and ¼ teaspoon pepper. Cover the pan and cook for about 8 minutes until the chard is soft.

* Uncover the pan and cook for a further 5 minutes or until most of the liquid has evaporated, stirring occasionally. Add the cornstarch and cook, stirring, for about 3 minutes until the sauce thickens. Remove pan from the heat, stir in the pine nuts and then taste and adjust the seasoning, adding more salt if necessary.

* Preheat the oven to 400°F (200°C). Lightly oil a roasting pan. Stuff an equal amount of the Swiss chard mixture into the belly of each fish. Place the stuffed fish in the roasting pan, drizzle with a bit of olive oil and season with salt and pepper. Sprinkle some extra rose petals over the fish and then bake for about 10 minutes until they are nicely cooked. Serve immediately.

Essaouira couscous

Essaouira is a charming coastal town in the south of Morocco. During our honeymoon, my husband, Zayd, and I spent a few days there, enjoying the freshest seafood in front of the most beautiful views. Although couscous is commonly cooked with meat in Morocco, fish couscous is actually a speciality of Essaouira and lots of Moroccans travel there just to enjoy it. This recipe is appropriate for all occasions and at any time of the year: on cold days the sweetness makes it hearty and comforting, and in the summer fish is always a good idea! Don't be tempted to cut the fish into small pieces when preparing it because it will break up while cooking. So keep the bream whole if you can, or cut them in half if they are too big to fit in your pan.

6 x 10.5 oz sea breams, cleaned, gutted and heads removed

3 tablespoons olive oil

2 large onions, sliced

2 tomatoes, deseeded and chopped into large chunks

3.5 oz celery, chopped

1 teaspoon ground turmeric

1 teaspoon ground ginger

¾ teaspoon salt

½ teaspoon ground black pepper

2 cups fish or vegetable stock

1⅔ cups water

1 bunch of fresh cilantro, tied together with kitchen string

10.5 oz turnips, peeled and cut into wedges

10.5 oz carrots, peeled, halved lengthways and cut into 2 inch lengths

¾ cup raisins

14 oz can chickpeas, rinsed and drained

7 oz baby zucchini, or regular zucchini cut into 2 inch lengths

2 red bell peppers, cored, deseeded and quartered

2⅓ cups couscous, cooked according to the packet instructions and seasoned with a bit of salt and olive oil

Marinade

2 tablespoons olive oil

1 teaspoon ground turmeric

1 teaspoon ground cumin

1 teaspoon ground ginger

1 teaspoon salt

½ teaspoon ground black pepper

* Mix all the ingredients for the marinade together in a large bowl. Add the bream making sure that the fish are fully covered by the marinade. Cover the bowl with plastic wrap and leave to marinate in the fridge until ready to use.

* Heat the olive oil in a large saucepan over medium heat. Add the onions, cover the pan and leave to cook for about 10 minutes until they are soft and translucent, stirring occasionally. Add the tomatoes, celery, turmeric, ginger, salt and pepper and cook, uncovered, for about 5 minutes, stirring occasionally, until the tomatoes and celery start to soften.

* Pour in the stock and water, add the cilantro bouquet and bring to a boil over high heat. Cover the pan, reduce the heat to medium-low and leave to simmer gently for 30 minutes to create a nice broth.

Continued on the next page...

* Add the marinated sea bream to the broth and bring to a boil over high heat. Re-cover the pan, reduce the heat to medium-low and simmer for about 12 minutes until the fish is cooked.

* Use tongs to carefully remove the fish from the pan and set aside. Discard the cilantro bouquet.

* Add the turnips, carrots and raisins to the broth and bring back to a boil over high heat. Re-cover the pan, reduce the heat to medium-low and simmer for 10 minutes. Then add the chickpeas, zucchini and red bell peppers. If the vegetables aren't covered with the broth at this stage, give the contents of the pan a good stir to distribute evenly, and if it's still the case, add just enough water to almost cover the vegetables. Bring to a boil over high heat, then re-cover the pan, reduce the heat to medium-low and simmer for about 15 minutes until all the vegetables are cooked.

* Remove the pan from the heat and gently return the fish to the broth. Re-cover the pan and leave for 5 minutes for the fish to warm up. To serve, place the warm couscous on a plate and top with the fish, vegetables, chickpeas and broth.

Tangier bastila cigars with labneh & turmeric sauce

Bastila usually comes in a circular shape, but I love to make cigars with my seafood-filled filo pastry — probably because it's much easier to dip a cigar in the delicious labneh and turmeric sauce! This *bastila* is a speciality of Tangier in the north of Morocco where the supply of seafood is abundant all year long. I have tried many versions of this traditional Moroccan dish, and while they are all remarkably tasty, every seafood *bastila* tastes different from the other. My mom and I have a constant debate about whether or not cinnamon should be added to a seafood *bastila* — I am Team Cinnamon (obviously!), and she isn't. But interestingly, she loves my seafood *bastila* cigars so much that she can't help eating up the last of them every single time I serve them. And I don't blame her! Filled with seafood goodness and tasting incredibly Moorish, these cigars have a massive knockout factor — perfect for serving as a part of a mezze or as a starter.

◄━━━━━►

⅓ cup unsalted butter

2 large onions, chopped

3 garlic cloves, peeled and crushed

2 teaspoons paprika

2 teaspoons ground cumin

¼ teaspoon ground cinnamon

1 teaspoon salt, or more to taste

½ teaspoon ground black pepper

generous pinch of cayenne pepper, or more to taste

7 oz skinless cod fillet, chopped into ¾ inch pieces

7 oz uncooked peeled prawns, chopped into ¾ inch pieces

7 oz cleaned squid tubes, chopped into ¾ inch pieces

3.5 oz dried rice vermicelli, cooked according to the packet instructions, drained and cut into ¾ inch pieces

2 small preserved lemons (2 oz; *see* page 9 for homemade), flesh and rind finely chopped

½ cup flat-leaf parsley, finely chopped

2½ tablespoons lemon juice, or more to taste

9.5 oz filo pastry sheets

1 egg, beaten

Labneh & turmeric sauce

¾ cup labneh or Greek yogurt

1 teaspoon ground turmeric

2 tablespoons lemon juice

2 teaspoons clear honey

Continued on the next page...

* Melt 2 tablespoons of the butter in a large skillet over a medium heat. Add the onions, garlic, paprika, cumin, cinnamon, salt, black pepper and cayenne pepper and cook for about 15 minutes until the onions are lightly golden, stirring occasionally. Then add the cod, prawns and squid and cook for about 4 minutes, stirring occasionally, until the prawns turn pink and the cod and squid are cooked through.

* Stir in the vermicelli, preserved lemons, parsley and lemon juice and cook over medium-low heat for about 5 minutes until there is no more liquid left in the pan. Taste and adjust the seasoning, adding more lemon juice, salt and cayenne pepper if necessary. Transfer the mixture to a bowl and leave to cool to room temperature. You can start assembling the cigars once the filling has cooled; a warm filling will moisten or may damage the filo pastry. Alternatively, cover the filling bowl with plastic wrap and keep in the fridge until ready to use.

* Preheat the oven to 400°F (200°C). Line a cookie sheet with parchment paper.

* Melt the remaining butter in a microwave or in a small saucepan on the stovetop.

* Divide the filling into 12 equal-sized portions. Use a sharp knife to cut the filo pastry sheets into 12 squares of about 9½ inches. Keep them covered with a dish towel to prevent them from drying out. Lay a filo square on a work surface and brush it with melted butter.

* Place a portion of seafood filling near the side of the pastry closest to you, leaving about 1 inch clear at either end. Fold the left and right sides over the filling to seal it in, then fold the closest side over the filling and roll tightly away from you to create a compact cigar. Place the rolled cigar on the lined cookie sheet and brush with the beaten egg. Repeat until you have used up all the filling. Bake the *bastila* for 20–25 minutes or until golden.

* Meanwhile, mix all the ingredients for the labneh and turmeric sauce in a serving bowl until smooth. Serve the cigars piping hot with the sauce on the side.

Merguez-stuffed squid in tomato sauce

To celebrate the end of my single life, my childhood friends Nilgun and Emna took me to the Cinque Terre on the Italian Riviera. One meal during this trip was particularly memorable: squid stuffed with ground meat laying on a bed of tomato sauce and al dente spaghetti. I asked the chef what the ground meat was seasoned with and, to my recollection, the ingredients he mentioned sounded a lot like what my parents use for their merguez sausages. The rest is history.

Merguez stuffing

2 tablespoons fennel seeds

2 tablespoons cumin seeds

2 tablespoons coriander seeds

½ lb ground lamb, 20% fat

½ lb ground beef, 20% fat

4 garlic cloves, peeled and crushed

⅓ cup fresh cilantro, finely chopped

½ cup fresh white breadcrumbs

2 tablespoons paprika

1 tablespoon superfine sugar

1 tablespoon dried mint

1 teaspoon salt, or more to taste

½ teaspoon cayenne pepper

½ teaspoon ground black pepper

Tomato sauce

2 tablespoons olive oil

1 large onion, chopped

2 garlic cloves, peeled and chopped

1 teaspoon paprika

1 teaspoon dried oregano

1 teaspoon superfine sugar

½ teaspoon ground cumin

½ teaspoon salt

¼ teaspoon smoked paprika

14 oz can chopped tomatoes

⅓ cup frozen peas

6 medium squid, about 4.5 oz each, cleaned, tentacles removed

pasta, couscous or crusty bread, to serve

* Toast the fennel, cumin and coriander seeds in a dry skillet over medium heat for about 3 minutes or until fragrant. Transfer to a pestle and mortar, spice or coffee grinder to roughly grind them.

* Place all the ingredients for the merguez stuffing in a large bowl along with the ground spices and use your hands to mix them together. Fill the squid tubes with the stuffing until about two-thirds full, making sure that they are tightly stuffed by packing the stuffing down firmly as you go. Secure each squid tube closed with a wooden toothpick. Place in the fridge until ready to use.

* To make the tomato sauce, heat the olive oil in a large saucepan over medium heat. Add the onion, cover the pan and cook for about 10 minutes or until soft and translucent, stirring occasionally.

Stir in the garlic, paprika, oregano, sugar, cumin, salt and smoked paprika, cover the pan and cook, stirring occasionally, for 5 minutes.

* Stir in the tomatoes and bring to a boil over high heat. Quickly add the stuffed squid, then re-cover the pan, reduce the heat to medium-low and leave to simmer gently for about 30 minutes or until the squid is tender and the stuffing is cooked and firm. If it looks like there isn't enough liquid in the pan at any point during the cooking process, add a few tablespoons of water.

* Throw in the peas and gently stir them into the sauce, then leave to cook for about 3 minutes or until tender. Serve immediately with pasta, couscous or crusty bread.

Monkfish tagine with apricots, dates & fennel

This tagine is my "guaranteed success" meal when I am hosting a dinner party for a group of people I don't know very well. So far, I haven't come across anyone who doesn't love this wonderful tagine. It is incredibly tasty but also healthy, packed with nutritious ingredients and naturally sweetened. Enjoy with a warm side of fluffy couscous.

4 tablespoons olive oil

2 large onions, sliced

2 large fennel bulbs, about ½ lb each, stalks discarded, thinly sliced

¾ cup vegetable stock

4 garlic cloves, peeled and crushed

1 teaspoon ground coriander

1 teaspoon ground cumin

1 teaspoon ground ginger

½ teaspoon ground turmeric

¾ teaspoon salt, or more to taste

½ teaspoon smoked paprika

¼ teaspoon ground black pepper

5.5 oz pitted soft dried dates (any type), chopped

¾ cup dried apricots, plus extra to garnish

2 lb 4 oz skinned and filleted monkfish tail, sliced into 2½ inch pieces

fresh cilantro leaves, to garnish

couscous, to serve

* Heat the olive oil in a large saucepan over medium heat and add the onions and fennel. Cover the pan, reduce the heat to medium-low and leave to cook gently for about 25 minutes, stirring occasionally, until they are soft and translucent.

* Stir in all the remaining ingredients except the monkfish and cilantro leaves. Bring to a boil over high heat, then reduce the heat to medium-low, re-cover the pan and simmer gently for 1 hour to obtain a nice broth. If it looks like there isn't enough liquid in the pan at any point during the cooking process, add a few tablespoons of water.

* Add the monkfish to the pan, re-cover and cook for 17–20 minutes until it is cooked through. Taste and adjust the seasoning, adding salt if necessary. Garnish with chopped dried apricots and cilantro leaves and serve immediately with a side of couscous.

Chermoula crumbed cod

This recipe is perfect when you're craving breaded fish but you still want to eat healthy. It's also perfect when you want to prepare something special but have little time available. Children and adults absolutely love it and always ask for a second portion. I recommend serving it with wilted greens and a dollop of mayonnaise or Greek yogurt.

4 skinless cod fillets, about 5 oz each
olive oil, for drizzling
juice of 1 lemon
salt and pepper
lemon wedges, to serve

Chermoula crumb

2 cups fresh white breadcrumbs
½ cup fresh cilantro, finely chopped
½ cup flat-leaf parsley, finely chopped
handful of mint leaves, finely chopped
3 tablespoons olive oil
3 garlic cloves, peeled and crushed
finely grated zest of 1 lemon
1 tablespoon lemon juice
2 teaspoons ground cumin
2 teaspoons paprika
½ teaspoon salt, or more to taste

* Preheat the oven to 400°F (200°C).

* Mix all the ingredients for the chermoula crumb together in a bowl, then taste and adjust the seasoning, adding salt if necessary.

* Place the cod fillets in a roasting pan, then drizzle with olive oil and lemon juice and season with salt and pepper on both sides. Sprinkle the chermoula crumb mixture on top of the fillets.

* Bake for 12–15 minutes or until the fish is cooked and the crumb is golden. Serve immediately with lemon wedges.

Plaice en papillote with honey, glazed grapefruit, leeks & capers

I make this recipe when I crave a refreshingly tasty meal but am not really in the mood to cook up a storm; minimum effort for maximum flavor is definitely my favorite kind of math. This dish tastes just as good as it looks, or probably better — the uncommon combination of wilted leeks and honey-glazed grapefruit slices is definitely a winner.

2 pink grapefruit

2 tablespoons olive oil, plus extra for drizzling

2 leeks, trimmed, cleaned and thinly sliced

3 garlic cloves, peeled and crushed

4¼ teaspoons unsalted butter

3 tablespoons clear honey

2 tablespoons superfine sugar

¼ teaspoon ground cinnamon

4 plaice fillets, about 5.5 oz each

4 tablespoons capers

salt and pepper

* Preheat the oven to 400°F (200°C).

* Cut a slice off the top and bottom of each grapefruit to reveal the flesh. Stand the grapefruit upright on a work surface and, cutting from top to bottom, remove the peel and white pith. Cut the fruit into thick slices and set aside.

* Heat the olive oil in a large skillet over medium heat. Add the leeks, cover the pan and leave to cook for about 12 minutes until soft, stirring occasionally. Uncover the pan, add the garlic and ½ teaspoon salt and cook for 3 minutes, stirring occasionally.

* Remove the leeks from the skillet and set aside. Melt the butter in the same skillet over medium heat, add the honey, sugar and cinnamon and stir until the sugar has melted. Remove the skillet from the heat and set aside for 1–2 minutes to allow the glaze to thicken slightly. Add the grapefruit slices

to the skillet and flip them over to make sure that both sides are covered with the glaze.

* Cut 4 pieces of parchment paper large enough to wrap around the plaice fillets. Fold each piece of paper in half and place a fish fillet to one side of the fold, drizzle with olive oil and season with salt and pepper on both sides. Top each fillet with a portion of the leeks, a couple glazed grapefruit slices and a tablespoon of capers. Fold the opposite side of the paper over the fish and fold all the open sides over tightly to seal the edges, making sure that there is enough space inside the parcel for the steam to circulate and cook the fish.

* Place the parcels on a cookie sheet and bake for about 10 minutes or until the fish is cooked through. Serve immediately.

My father's turmeric seafood soup

When I was 13, the whole family — me, my parents and my brothers — went on a road trip through northern Morocco. When we returned, my father started raving about this soup he and my mom had eaten in a small restaurant in Tangier while my brothers and I were playing video games. "Can you replicate it, Amal?" I heard him ask my mom this question at least a dozen times before she finally started experimenting. It quickly became my father's favorite and a classic in my parents' home. It's so incredibly tasty, healthy and easy to prepare. Who can resist?

━━◆━━

2 tablespoons olive oil

3 garlic cloves, peeled and crushed

1 teaspoon ground turmeric

¾ teaspoon salt, or more to taste

¼ teaspoon ground black pepper

7 oz skinless flaky white fish fillet, such as cod,
cut into large chunks

2 cups vegetable stock

1¼ cups water

14 oz live clams

7 oz cleaned squid tubes, sliced into rings

½ cup flat-leaf parsley, finely chopped

━━◆━━

* Heat the olive oil in a large saucepan over medium heat. Add the garlic, then stir in the turmeric, salt and pepper and cook for 3 minutes, stirring occasionally. Throw in the fish pieces and cook for 5 minutes, turning them occasionally.

* Pour in the stock and water and bring to a boil over high heat. Cover the pan, reduce the heat to low and leave to simmer gently for 10 minutes until the fish is just cooked through.

* Meanwhile, prepare your clams. Sort through them and chuck out any with damaged shells or that don't shut when lightly tapped on a surface. Scrub the shells clean. Rinse thoroughly under cold running water and drain.

* Add the clams and squid rings to the pan, re-cover and leave to cook for about 5 minutes until the clams have opened and the squid is tender. Discard any clams that have failed to open. Taste and adjust the seasoning, adding more salt if necessary. Add the parsley and give the contents of the pan a good stir. Serve immediately.

Ras el hanout, crab & roasted cauliflower soup

Crab has a very distinctive taste and I find that cauliflower perfectly balances its pungent and sweet flavor. Adding some ras el hanout brings warmth and a little scent to this creamy soup. Every time I serve this, I'm told that it tastes extremely special and seems very fancy, which goes to prove that all you need to impress your guests is just a few quality ingredients!

1 lb 5 oz cauliflower, broken into florets
3 shallots, roughly chopped
2 tablespoons olive oil, plus extra to serve
3 garlic cloves, peeled and crushed
½ teaspoon salt, or more to taste
2 cups chicken or vegetable stock

1 cup water
1 teaspoon ras el hanout (*see* page 9 for homemade)
7 oz cooked crabmeat, half brown and half white meat
¾ cup heavy cream
pumpkin seeds, to serve

* Preheat the oven to 400°F (200°C). Toss the cauliflower florets and shallots with the olive oil, garlic and salt in a roasting pan, then spread them out in the pan. Roast for about 30 minutes until tender and golden.

* Remove from the oven and transfer the roasted cauliflower and shallots to a large saucepan. Pour in the stock and water, add the ras el hanout and stir to combine. Bring to a boil over high heat, then cover the pan, reduce the heat to medium-low and leave to simmer gently for 30 minutes.

* Purée the soup in the pan using a immersion blender, or transfer the soup to a blender and blend until smooth, then return it to the pan. Add the crabmeat and cream and stir to combine. Taste and adjust the seasoning, adding more salt if necessary. Leave the soup to heat through over medium heat for a few minutes, then serve topped with a drizzle of olive oil and a sprinkling of pumpkin seeds.

Red chermoula prawn & scallop skewers

I like to think that my red chermoula is a romantic version of the classic chermoula (*see* page 142); sweeter, less piquant and with just the right amount of aroma and smokiness. It works particularly well with seafood and poultry. Scallops come in a variety of sizes, so depending on the type you buy for this recipe, you may end up with two or more scallops on each of your skewers.

½ lb shucked and cleaned medium scallops without roe (coral)
½ lb uncooked, peeled large prawns

Red chermoula (makes 3 oz)

3 tablespoons olive oil
½ cup fresh cilantro, finely chopped
2 garlic cloves, peeled and finely chopped
1 tablespoon red wine vinegar
1 tablespoon tomato purée
1 tablespoon clear honey
1 teaspoon paprika
½ teaspoon smoked paprika
½ teaspoon salt, or more to taste

* Stir all the ingredients for the red chermoula together in a large bowl until smooth. Add the scallops and prawns and gently combine them with the marinade. Cover the bowl with plastic wrap and leave to marinate in the fridge for 2–12 hours.

* Thread the prawns and scallops on to skewers. Preheat a skillet or griddle or a barbecue to a high heat. Place the kebabs on your pan or barbecue and cook for about 4 minutes, turning regularly, until the prawns turn pink and the scallops are just cooked through. Serve immediately.

6
BREADS

Bread

For Moroccans, bread is a cherished food, so much so that throwing away even a piece of it is considered an offence and an insult to those deprived of nourishment.

I grew up in a home where we rarely bought bread; most of the time, we would bake it. I think the main reason why my parents, along with the majority of Moroccans, have a special relationship with bread is because tagines are exclusively enjoyed with bread. In fact, if you are lucky enough to spend some time in a Moroccan home, you will notice that on the side of your tagine there won't be any couscous or rice — only bread. And since tagines are fundamental to Moroccan cuisine, bread is inevitably eaten on a daily basis and often a couple times a day.

There are countless kinds of breads in Morocco, but the most common is the basic version of *khobz* (*see* page 172), which translates from Arabic to "bread," a relatively thin but not flat disc-shaped loaf. The bread is beautifully golden and crunchy on the outside and contrastingly soft and pillowy on the inside. Its consistency is ideal for scooping pieces of meat or vegetables and absorbing the sauce of tagines.

I will never forget the first time I went to a Moroccan restaurant in London and my tagine arrived served with a side of herbed couscous. I was very surprised — well, to be honest, quite shocked. Back then, it somehow felt wrong and I wasn't sure if I should just go ahead and eat my tagine with the couscous or refuse to betray my cultural customs and ask the waiter for some bread. I ended up eating the tagine with the couscous and I loved it! Sometimes embracing new concepts can feel odd at first, but in this case, it didn't take long for me to get used to eating my tagine with couscous.

Ever since, I've been enjoying most of my tagines with a whole range of different grains such as quinoa, barley, buckwheat and even bulgur. Bread is always an option, and a very dear one, but I totally recommend being adventurous and having your tagine with any side dish that makes you happy.

Wholemeal mahrash bread

This bread (*see* photograph on pages 170-1) is called *mahrash* in Moroccan Arabic, meaning "coarse," because of its rough texture and is commonly sold in the souks during the winter. In order to give *mahrash* its special consistency and appearance, barley grits — toasted and cracked pearl barley — are sprinkled all over the loaf before baking (barley is an old-fashioned cereal extensively used in Morocco to make couscous, porridge and bread). My favorite part of this recipe is at the very beginning when you toast the barley pearls; they turn golden and release a delicate sweet scent of honey and flowers. Truly enchanting.

½ cup pearl barley
1 tablespoon dried active yeast
1 tablespoon superfine sugar
2½ cups wholemeal flour

¾ cup all-purpose flour, plus extra if needed and for dusting
1 teaspoon salt
3 tablespoons olive oil, plus extra for oiling
¾–1 cup warm water

* Toast the pearl barley in a dry skillet over medium high heat for about 5 minutes or until fragrant. Transfer the toasted barley to a food processor and process for a few seconds to break them up. Pass the cracked barley through a sieve and discard the flour, reserving the white bits left in the sieve, which are the barley grits. Set aside until ready to use.

* In a small bowl, mix the dried yeast with ¼ teaspoon of the sugar and 1 tablespoon warm water using a fork. Leave the yeast to activate for about 5 minutes or until the mixture is foamy.

* Mix the flours, remaining sugar and salt together in a large bowl. Pour in the olive oil, yeast mixture and ¾ cup of the warm water, then use your hands to mix the ingredients together to form a soft dough. The dough should feel quite sticky. If your dough is too dry, gradually add a little extra warm water, a tablespoon at a time, until you obtain the right consistency. If it's too sticky, add a bit more all-purpose flour.

* Lightly dust a surface with all-purpose flour and knead the dough for about 10 minutes until smooth and elastic — to check it is kneaded enough, press it with your finger and it should bounce back.

* Oil 2 cookie sheets. Divide the dough into quarters and form each quarter into a ball. Place 2 balls in the center of each oiled cookie sheet, leaving at least 3 inches between them to allow enough room for flattening and rising. Cover with plastic wrap and leave the dough to rest in a warm place for 15 minutes.

* Use your fingers to lightly rub the top of the dough with water and generously sprinkle all over with the barley grits. Using your hands, flatten each ball into a disc ½ inch thick, making sure that the barley grits are stuck to the top of the dough. Cover with plastic wrap and leave the dough to rise for about 1 hour until it doubles in size — it may need longer if it is left in a cold room.

* Preheat the oven to 430°F (220°C). Once the dough has risen, use a sharp knife to score a cross on top of each loaf. Bake for about 27 minutes (but begin checking for doneness after 22 minutes) until golden on top and on the underside, and the bread sounds hollow when you gently tap it on the bottom. Remove from the oven, transfer to a wire rack and leave to cool for 10 minutes before serving.

Khobz — Everyday bread

Khobz is the Holy Grail of Moroccan culture and gastronomy. We serve this bread for breakfast and alongside every meal. When Moroccans mention *khobz*, they are usually referring to its most classic form: a plain white round loaf of bread. Its texture is exceptionally suitable for tagines: crunchy on top yet thick and pillowy on the inside, which allows for scooping up the tagine and its juices. You will never come across a traditional Moroccan dining table that isn't adorned with golden pieces of *khobz*.

2 teaspoons dried active yeast

1 tablespoon superfine sugar

2⅓ cups all-purpose flour, plus extra if needed

⅔ cup semolina, plus extra for dusting

1 teaspoon salt

3 tablespoons olive oil, plus extra for oiling

⅔–¾ cup warm water

* In a small bowl, mix the dried yeast with ¼ teaspoon of the sugar and 1 tablespoon warm water using a fork. Leave the yeast to activate for about 5 minutes or until the mixture is foamy.

* Mix the flour, semolina, remaining sugar and salt together in a large bowl. Pour in the olive oil, yeast mixture and ⅔ cup of the warm water, then use your hands to mix the ingredients together to form a soft dough. The dough should feel a bit tacky but not too sticky. If your dough is too dry, gradually add a little extra warm water, a tablespoon at a time, until you obtain the right consistency. If it's too sticky, add a bit more all-purpose flour.

* Lightly dust a work surface with semolina and knead the dough for about 10 minutes or until smooth and elastic — to check that it has been kneaded enough, press it with your finger and it should bounce back.

* Oil 2 cookie sheets. Divide the dough in half and form each half into a ball. Place one ball in the center of each oiled cookie sheet, cover with plastic wrap and leave the dough to rest in a warm place for 15 minutes.

* Use your fingers to lightly rub the top of the dough with water and generously dust all over with semolina. Using your hands, flatten each ball into a disc ½ inch thick, cover with plastic wrap and leave the dough to rise for about 1 hour or until it doubles in size — it may need longer if it is left in a cold room.

* Preheat the oven to 430°F (220°C). Once the dough has risen, use a sharp knife to score a cross on top of each loaf. Bake for about 27 minutes (but begin checking for doneness after 22 minutes) until golden on top and on the underside, and the bread sounds hollow when you gently tap it on the bottom. Remove from the oven, transfer to a wire rack and leave to cool for 10 minutes before serving.

Mkhamer — Skillet bread

Skillet bread, *mkhamer*, *matlouh*, *meltoua*, large *batbout* — this bread has so many names, it was a struggle to decide what to call this recipe. If you've tried a similar bread in Morocco but you don't recognize this recipe title, it's still very likely to have been the same bread. What its proper name is really doesn't matter; all you need to know is that it's a soft and beautifully airy skillet-fried semolina bread. If you or your children don't like bread crust, let me introduce you to your new favorite bread — so pillowy, you could stack the loaves up and take a nap.

────────

1 teaspoon dried active yeast
1¼ teaspoons superfine sugar
¾ cup all-purpose flour, plus extra if needed
⅔ cup semolina, plus extra for dusting
½ teaspoon salt
1 tablespoon olive oil, plus extra for oiling
½–⅔ cup warm water

────────

* In a small bowl, mix the dried yeast and ¼ teaspoon of the sugar with 1 tablespoon warm water using a fork. Leave the yeast to activate for about 5 minutes or until the mixture is foamy.

* Mix the flour, semolina, remaining sugar and salt together in a large bowl. Pour in the olive oil, yeast mixture and ½ cup warm water, then use your hands to mix the ingredients together to form a soft dough. The dough should feel slightly sticky. If your dough is too dry, gradually add a little extra warm water, a tablespoon at a time, until you obtain the right consistency. If it's too sticky, add a bit more all-purpose flour.

* Lightly dust a work surface with semolina and knead the dough for about 10 minutes until smooth and elastic — to check that it has been kneaded enough, press it with your finger and it should bounce back. Divide the dough in half and shape each into a round loaf. Cover each loaf with plastic wrap and leave to rest in a warm place for 15 minutes.

* Using your hands, flatten each loaf into a disc ¼ inch thick and dust both sides with semolina. Place the discs on a tray or work surface in a warm place, leaving at least 2 inches between each loaf to allow enough room for rising. Cover the discs with plastic wrap and leave to rise for about 1 hour until they double in size — they may need longer if they are left in a cold room.

* Lightly oil a skillet, ideally heavy based, and preheat over medium heat. Gently place a loaf in the skillet and cook, turning several times, for about 6 minutes on each side until golden. Remove from the skillet and place on a wire rack while you cook the other loaf in the same way. Leave the bread to cool for a few minutes before serving.

Seeded harcha

At the top of the Moroccan breakfast essentials pyramid, you will indisputably find *baghrir* (*see* page 44), *msemen* (*see* page 178) and *harcha*. A bit like a scone, *harcha* is at the crossroads between a bread and a cake, and also like a scone, you will find endless versions of *harcha*. They are deliciously tasty and rich, and their consistency is delicately soft on the inside and lightly crisp on the outside. I love my seeded version because it is so healthy and versatile — you can enjoy them with either sweet or savoury fillings, although I must admit that I have a preference for ricotta cheese and strawberry jam or honey. If you want to make plain *harcha*, simply leave out the seeds.

¾ cup semolina
2½ tablespoons poppy seeds
2½ tablespoons sesame seeds
2½ tablespoons sunflower seeds
1½ tablespoons superfine sugar
½ teaspoon baking powder
¼ teaspoon salt
2¾ tablespoons unsalted butter, softened
8–10 teaspoons milk (any type)
olive oil, for oiling

* Mix the semolina, 1 tablespoon of the poppy seeds, 1 tablespoon of the sesame seeds, 1 tablespoon of the sunflower seeds, the sugar, baking powder and salt in a bowl. Add the softened butter and use your hands to combine it with the dry ingredients until you have a slightly moist mixture.

* Stir in about 4 teaspoons of the milk and mix again. Keep gradually stirring in enough of the remaining milk until you obtain a dough consistency — the amount of milk needed will depend on the type of semolina you are using. Let the *harcha* dough rest for 15 minutes to allow the semolina to absorb the milk.

* Divide the dough into 5 equal-sized balls. Mix the remaining seeds together in a small bowl, then sprinkle them all over a work surface. Place each ball of dough on top of the seed mixture and flatten into a disc ½ inch thick, making sure that both sides are coated with seeds.

* Lightly oil a skillet, ideally heavy based, and preheat over medium heat. Add the *harcha* to the hot pan and cook, turning several times, for about 4 minutes on each side or until golden and firm. Leave them to cool for 10 minutes before serving.

Almond msemen

Msemen, also known as *rghaeif*, is a soft, thin-layered skillet-fried bread. You will find plain, stuffed, sweet and savoury varieties of *msemen* everywhere in Morocco. This version, stuffed with almond paste, is incredibly satisfying and would make the perfect start to a day or a comforting end to a pleasant meal (*see* photo on page 180). For plain *msemen*, simply omit the almond paste.

1 cup, 3 tablespoons all-purpose flour
1 cup semolina, plus extra if needed
and for dusting
½ teaspoon salt
½ cup warm water
2 tablespoons vegetable oil,
plus extra for the dough and for oiling

Almond paste
¾ cup blanched almonds
¼ cup superfine sugar
generous pinch of ground cinnamon
pinch of salt
1½ tablespoons orange blossom water
2 teaspoons unsalted butter, softened

To serve
6 tablespoons clear honey
2 tablespoons toasted sesame seeds

* Place the flour, semolina, salt, warm water and vegetable oil in a large bowl, then use your hands to mix the ingredients together to form a soft, smooth dough. If the mixture is too dry to form a dough, gradually add an extra couple tablespoons of warm water, but if it's too sticky, add a bit more semolina. When your dough is nicely soft, lightly dust a work surface with semolina and knead the dough for about 8 minutes or until light and elastic.

* Divide the dough into 9 equal-sized pieces and form each into a ball. Lightly drizzle the balls with vegetable oil, cover with plastic wrap and leave to rest in a warm place for 30 minutes.

* Meanwhile, make the almond paste. Place all the almond paste ingredients in a food processor and process until you have a moist paste. This will take a bit of time — about 5 minutes, depending on the machine you are using. Remove the almond paste from the food processor, then divide it into 9 equal-sized pieces and form each into a ball.

* Once rested, take a ball of dough and pour about ½ teaspoon vegetable oil on top. Using your hands, flatten the dough as thinly as you can and form into a circle or square without damaging the dough.

* Take an almond paste ball and flatten it thinly with the palm of your hand, then immediately place it in the center of the dough circle or square. Fold the 2 sides of the dough over the almond paste in towards the center, then the top and bottom edges in, to roughly form a 3 inch circle or square. Place the *msemen* on a tray and use your fingers to lightly rub it with vegetable oil to avoid the dough from drying out. Repeat with the remaining dough and almond paste.

* Lightly oil a skillet, ideally heavy based, and preheat over medium heat. In the order in which you prepared them, place the first *msemen* on the work surface so the fold is underneath and flatten it with your hands to about ¼ inch thick. Gently transfer the flattened *msemen* to the hot skillet and cook, turning several times, for about 5 minutes or until golden on both sides and cooked through. Repeat with the remaining *msemen*.

* Serve the *msemen* warm, drizzled with the honey and sprinkled with the toasted sesame seeds.

Mlaoui

Reader, meet *mlaoui*, *msemen*'s (*see* page 178) rebellious younger brother. They are both made from the same dough and look extremely similar, but each is unique. *Mlaoui* is richer and a bit more complex, and its consistency is crispier and fluffier — in fact, it is probably the flakiest skillet-fried flatbread I have ever come across. The traditional topping for both *mlaoui* and *msemen* is a syrup made from equal parts melted butter and warm honey. A delightful Moroccan classic that can be served with anything, sweet or savoury.

1 cup, 3 tablespoons all-purpose flour,
plus extra for dusting
1 cup semolina, plus an extra 4 tablespoons
½ teaspoon salt
½–¾ cup warm water
5 tablespoons vegetable oil,
plus extra for drizzling and oiling
2 tablespoons unsalted butter, melted

To serve
butter
jam

* Mix the all-purpose flour, 1¼ cups semolina and salt together in a large bowl. Pour in ½ cup warm water and 2 tablespoons of the vegetable oil, then use your hands to mix the ingredients together to form a soft, smooth dough. If the mixture is too dry to form a dough, gradually add a little extra warm water, a tablespoon at a time, but if it's too sticky, add a bit more semolina. When your dough is nicely soft, lightly dust a work surface with all-purpose flour and knead the dough for about 8 minutes or until light and elastic.

* Divide the dough into 9 equal-sized pieces and form each into a ball. Lightly drizzle the balls with vegetable oil, cover with plastic wrap and leave to rest in a warm place for 30 minutes.

* Once the dough has rested, take a ball of dough and pour about ½ teaspoon melted butter on top. Using your hands, flatten the dough as thinly as you can and form into a circle or square without damaging the dough. Generously sprinkle the flattened dough with semolina, then fold the top and bottom edges of the dough in thirds to meet in the center to form a long rectangle. Lightly drizzle the long rectangle with more melted butter, sprinkle with more semolina and quickly roll it up like a rug to form a coil. Place the coil upright on a tray and lightly drizzle with vegetable oil to avoid the dough from drying out. Repeat with the remaining balls of dough.

* Lightly oil a skillet (ideally heavy based), and preheat over medium heat. In the order in which you prepared them, place the first *mlaoui* on the work surface and flatten it with your hands to about ¼ inch thick. Gently transfer the flattened *mlaoui* to the hot skillet and cook, turning several times, for about 5 minutes or until golden on both sides and cooked through. Repeat with the remaining *mlaoui*. Serve warm with butter and jam.

Opposite: Almond *msemen* (with honey and toasted sesame seeds) and *Mlaoui* (with butter and jam).

Khlii scones

Khlii is an incomparable filling for anything doughy or bread-like, so intensely packed with flavor and versatile that it has the ability to transform and enhance any dish or baked good effortlessly. My mom makes the absolute best *khlii* (*see* page 86 for her recipe), and every time she comes to visit me in London, we make a big batch for storing in the fridge and using as and when I want. One of my favorite ways of using *khlii* is in these rich scones, which have a beautiful crumbly texture and are packed with Moroccan flavors. Another must-try!

———

1¾ cups all-purpose flour, plus extra for dusting

2 teaspoons baking powder

¾ teaspoon salt

½ teaspoon baking soda

½ teaspoon ground cumin

½ teaspoon ground coriander

⅓ cup cold butter, cut into ⅓ inch cubes

7 oz Khlii (*see* page 86), cut into ⅓ inch pieces and drained of excess oil

½ cup buttermilk

1 egg yolk, for glazing

———

* Preheat the oven to 400°F (200°C). Line a cookie sheet with parchment paper.

* Mix the flour, baking powder, salt, baking soda, cumin and coriander together in a large bowl. Add the butter and rub in with your fingertips until the mixture looks like large, coarse breadcrumbs.

* Throw in the chopped khlii and use a large metal spoon to mix it into the flour mixture. Pour in the buttermilk and mix to form a dough. Gather the dough together with your hands and knead it for 30–60 seconds until soft and spongy — don't overknead, otherwise it will make the scones tough.

* Place the dough on a work surface dusted with flour and roughly roll it out into a circle ¾ inch thick. Cut the dough circle into 8 wedges and place them on the lined cookie sheet, leaving a bit of space between each. Brush the scones with the egg yolk and bake for 16–20 minutes or until they have risen and are golden brown on top. Serve warm or at room temperature.

Ghee, black olive & thyme bread rolls

In Morocco, ghee (also known as *smen*) is mainly used to enhance the taste of savoury foods such as bread, couscous and tagines. Interestingly, there are two kinds of *smen* in Morocco: one called *smen mdaweb*, which is exactly like ghee and prepared with clarified butter, and the other called *smen mleh*, made from fermented butter with a taste somewhat similar to blue cheese. At home, we use *smen mdaweb* for baking and sometimes to season and grease our couscous grains before serving them. I love using *smen* when I bake, as I find that it gives a beautiful yellow tone and an irresistible sweet-scented taste to my baked goods.

¼ cup ghee
2½ teaspoons dried active yeast
1 tablespoon superfine sugar
3¼ cups all-purpose flour, plus extra if needed and for dusting

2 tablespoons finely chopped thyme leaves
1 teaspoon salt
⅔–¾ cup warm water
⅓ cup drained pitted black olives, finely chopped
olive oil, for oiling

* Melt the ghee in a microwave or in a small saucepan on the stovetop, then leave it to cool until it feels warm to touch but no longer hot.

* Meanwhile, in a small bowl, mix the dried yeast with ¼ teaspoon of the sugar and 1 tablespoon warm water using a fork. Leave the yeast to activate for about 5 minutes until the mixture is foamy.

* Mix the flour, the remaining sugar, thyme and salt together in a large bowl. Pour in the ghee, yeast mixture and ⅔ cup of the warm water, then use your hands to mix the ingredients together to form a soft dough. The dough should feel slightly sticky. If your dough is too dry, gradually add a little extra warm water, a tablespoon at a time, until you obtain the right consistency. If it's too sticky, add a bit more flour.

* Lightly dust a work surface with flour and knead the dough for about 10 minutes until smooth and elastic — to check that it has been kneaded enough, press it with your finger and it should

bounce back. Once you are happy with the consistency of the dough, add the chopped olives, making sure that they are evenly distributed. Form the dough into a ball and place in a lightly oiled bowl. Cover with plastic wrap and leave to rise for about 1 hour until it doubles in size — it may need longer if left in a cold room.

* Divide the dough into 8 equal-sized pieces and shape each into a ball. Place them on 2 cookie sheets, leaving about 2 inches between each ball. Cover with plastic wrap and leave the rolls to rise for about 1 hour until they almost double in size.

* Preheat the oven to 400°F (200°C). Once the rolls have risen, bake for about 25 minutes (but begin checking for doneness after 20 minutes) until browned on top and on the underside, and the rolls sound hollow when you gently tap them on the bottom. Transfer to a wire rack and leave to cool for 10 minutes before serving.

Cumin & buttermilk cornbread

I discovered cornbread a few years ago on a trip to New York and instantly adored it. Its light, fluffy texture and yet coarse consistency makes this bread one of a kind. Given my non-existent American entourage back home, it took some time for me to perfect the recipe. But after a few trials, I was delighted to finally crack the code. Here, I am giving a sweet and perfumed twist to a classic cornbread with toasted cumin seeds. It's a quick one-bowl recipe ready in 40 minutes that requires minimal kitchen equipment, so it would be a crime not to try it! Be sure to use cornmeal and not cornstarch. Sometimes cornmeal is labelled as polenta, but don't use instant polenta for this recipe, as you won't obtain the right result.

1 tablespoon cumin seeds, plus an extra 1 teaspoon for sprinkling

½ cup unsalted butter, melted

½ cup superfine sugar

2 eggs, beaten

1 cup buttermilk

1 cup cornmeal

1 cup, 3 tablespoons all-purpose flour

½ teaspoon baking soda

½ teaspoon salt

* Preheat the oven to 400°F (200°C). Line an 8 inch square baking pan with parchment paper.

* Toast the cumin seeds in a dry skillet over medium heat for about 2 minutes until fragrant. Remove from the pan and set aside.

* Pour the melted butter into a large bowl, add the sugar and mix together until foamy. Add the beaten eggs and stir until well combined. Pour in the buttermilk and whisk until well blended. Finally, add the cornmeal, flour, baking soda, salt and toasted cumin seeds and stir until well combined.

* Transfer the batter to the lined pan and sprinkle the extra cumin seeds all over. Bake for about 27 minutes (but begin checking for doneness after 22 minutes) until golden on top and a toothpick inserted into the center comes out dry.

* Remove from the oven, then transfer the cornbread from the pan to a wire rack to cool for 10 minutes before serving.

Amlou rolls

My love for all things *amlou* has taken me to many places, and I can assure you that this recipe is my favorite destination. These rolls are so rich and scrumptious, they could easily be served as a dessert, but I could easily have them for breakfast, lunch and dinner. Which is why I thought classifying them in the bread section made more sense. *Amlou* is a paste made of ground almonds, honey and argan oil and happens to be one of the easiest things to prepare. And don't worry if you don't have argan oil — walnut oil will do the job. These rolls taste like a bunch of cinnamon rolls that travelled to Casablanca and adopted the local customs; they look very Western, but there's something very Moroccan about them.

Dough
½ cup unsalted butter
2¼ teaspoons dried active yeast
¼ cup superfine sugar
1 tablespoon warm water
¾–1 cup warm full-fat milk
1 large egg
3½ cups all-purpose flour, plus extra if needed and for dusting
½ teaspoon salt
vegetable oil, for oiling
1 egg, beaten, for glazing

Filling
⅔ cup Amlou (*see page* 189)
2 tablespoons superfine sugar
1 teaspoon ground cinnamon

Glaze
⅓ cup confectioners' sugar
½ tablespoon milk
¼ teaspoon vanilla extract
pinch of salt

continued on page 188

* To make the dough, melt the butter in a microwave or in a saucepan on the stovetop, then leave it to cool until it feels warm to touch but no longer hot.

* Meanwhile, in a small bowl, mix the dried yeast with ¼ teaspoon of the sugar and the warm water using a fork. Leave the yeast to activate for about 5 minutes until the mixture is foamy.

* Pour the melted butter, ¾ cup of the warm milk, the yeast mixture and the egg into a bowl, then mix together until smooth.

* In another large bowl, mix the flour, remaining sugar and salt together.

* Add the egg and milk mixture to the flour mixture and use your hands to mix the ingredients together to form a soft dough. The dough should feel slightly sticky. If your dough is too dry, gradually add a little extra of the remaining warm milk, a tablespoon at a time, until you obtain the right consistency. If it's too sticky, add a bit more flour.

* Lightly dust a work surface with flour and knead the dough for about 8 minutes until smooth and elastic. Form the dough into a ball and place in a lightly oiled bowl. Cover with plastic wrap and

leave the dough to rise in a warm place for 30 minutes. Oil a 11 inch rectangular roasting pan (or 12 inch round baking pan) and line with parchment paper.

* Turn the dough out on the work surface lightly dusted with flour and roll it out to a rectangle 9 x 13 inches. Spread the *amlou* all over the dough, then sprinkle the sugar and cinnamon all over the *amlou*. Roll up the dough into a long log. Cut the log into 11 slices, 1 inch thick, and place in the prepared pan, leaving a bit of space between the rolls to allow them to expand. Cover with plastic wrap and leave to rise in a warm place for 30 minutes.

* Preheat the oven to 375°F (190°C). Brush the rolls with the beaten egg, then bake for 17–22 minutes or until cooked through and golden and a toothpick inserted in the centers comes out dry.

* Meanwhile, stir all the ingredients for the glaze together in a bowl until smooth.

* Once the rolls are baked, remove them from the oven, transfer them from the pan to a wire rack and leave to cool for 5 minutes. Drizzle the glaze over the rolls and serve.

Amlou

Amlou is a brown paste made by grinding roasted almonds and mixing them with honey and argan oil. It is commonly known as a speciality from the southwest of Morocco, one of only two regions in the world (the other being western Algeria) where argan trees are native. In Morocco, *amlou* is usually served for breakfast or afternoon tea with bread and pancakes. If you follow me online, you will be well acquainted with my love for all things *amlou*. I like adding it to smoothies, salads and pastries, but you can also serve it as a spread or dip, or on top of anything you fancy, such as fruit, *khobz* (*see* page 172), *msemen* (*see* page 178) and *baghrir* (*see* page 44). And don't forget to check out the recipe for my Amlou Rolls (*see* page 186). Make sure that you use skin-on almonds and not blanched almonds to get an authentic *amlou* result. It's traditionally quite runny rather than paste-like in consistency, but I like mine a little thicker so that I can use it as a spread. If you would prefer a thinner *amlou*, use the larger quantity of argan oil specified in the ingredients. If you can't find argan oil where you live, it would be a shame to miss out on a taste of *amlou*, so I recommend using walnut oil as a substitute.

◄———►

1¾ cup unblanched almonds
½–¾ cup argan oil (or walnut oil)
¼ cup clear honey, or more to taste
½ teaspoon salt

◄———►

* Preheat the oven to 400°F (200°C). Spread the almonds out on a cookie sheet and roast for 10–12 minutes until lightly golden, giving them a good stir halfway through to make sure that they roast evenly. Remove from the oven and leave the almonds until cool enough to handle.

* Tip the roasted almonds into a food processor and pulse until they are finely ground, but make sure not to overgrind them, otherwise they could turn into almond butter. With the motor running, gradually add your desired amount of oil, depending on the consistency of *amlou* you like, and process for a few seconds until smooth. Then add the honey and process again for a few seconds until combined.

* Store in an airtight container in a cool, dark place such as your kitchen cupboard for up to 1 month. Just remember to give it a good stir before serving.

Chocolate chip krachel

Krachel are rich sweet buns made with aniseed and sesame seeds. They are very popular in Morocco where you will find them in all kinds of bakeries and shops or in the souk sitting nicely on top of small carts. My mom and I unapologetically love chocolate, so when we make *krachel*, chocolate has to be involved. I love eating these warm, fresh from the oven, with salted butter. Make sure that you use whole aniseed and not ground aniseed for this recipe to achieve an authentic *krachel* result, and keep the buns in an airtight container to prevent them from drying out or store them in the freezer.

¼ cup unsalted butter
2½ tablespoons sesame seeds
2 teaspoons dried active yeast
¼ cup superfine sugar
1 tablespoon warm water
2 cups, 3 tablespoons all-purpose flour, plus extra if needed and for dusting
1 teaspoon aniseed

½ teaspoon salt
1 egg
⅓–½ cup warm full-fat milk
1½ tablespoons orange blossom water
½ cup dark chocolate chips or chunks
vegetable oil, for oiling
1 egg yolk, beaten

* Melt the butter in a microwave or in a small saucepan on the stovetop, then leave it to cool until it feels warm to touch but no longer hot. Toast the sesame seeds in a small, dry skillet over medium-high heat for about 6 minutes until golden brown, tossing occasionally. Set aside.

* In a small bowl, mix the dried yeast with ¼ teaspoon of the sugar and the measured warm water using a fork. Leave the yeast to activate for about 5 minutes until the mixture is foamy.

* Mix 2 tablespoons of the toasted sesame seeds, the remaining sugar, the flour, aniseed and salt together in a large bowl. In a separate bowl, whisk the melted butter, yeast mixture, egg, ⅓ cup warm milk and the orange blossom water together until smooth. Pour the egg and milk mixture into the flour mixture and use your hands to mix the ingredients together to form a soft dough. The dough should feel slightly sticky. If your dough is too dry, gradually add a little extra warm milk, a tablespoon at a time, until you obtain the right consistency. If it's too sticky, add a bit more flour.

* Lightly dust a work surface with flour and knead the dough for about 10 minutes until smooth and elastic — to check that it has been kneaded enough, press it with your finger and it should bounce back. Once you are happy with the consistency of the dough, add the chocolate chips or chunks, making sure that they are evenly distributed. Form the dough into a ball and place in a lightly oiled bowl. Cover with plastic wrap and leave to rise for about 45 minutes or until it almost doubles in size — it may need longer if left in a cold room.

* Divide the dough into 8 equal-sized pieces and shape each into a ball. Place them on a cookie sheet, leaving about 2 inches between each ball. Cover with plastic wrap and leave the buns to rise for about 30 minutes.

* Preheat the oven to 375°F (190°C). When ready to bake, brush the buns with the beaten egg yolk and sprinkle with the remaining toasted sesame seeds. Bake for about 17–20 minutes or until the *krachel* are golden brown and cooked through. Serve warm or at room temperature.

7
DESSERTS

Sellou — Moroccan edible cookie dough

When we were kids, my brothers' and my favorite ice cream was Häagen-Dazs' Cookie Dough. Each of us would always make sure we helped ourselves to the ice cream so that we could pick out the soft pieces of uncooked dough. That's what this ice cream was all about — we didn't care much about the ice cream itself. Obviously, we were familiar with cookie dough, and by familiar I mean obsessed, but we were never allowed to eat it raw. Our mom noticed our questionable obsession and satisfied it with *sellou*, also known as Moroccan edible cookie dough. *Sellou* is fascinating, as it uses a baking technique that I have never seen in any other country: roasting the flour. If you fancy a chocolate-chip cookie dough experience, just throw in some chocolate chips!

1 cup blanched almonds
1 cup sesame seeds
1 cup, 2 tablespoons all-purpose flour
1 teaspoon ground aniseed

½ tablespoon ground cinnamon
¼ teaspoon salt
¾ cup clear honey
1½ tablespoons butter, softened

* Preheat the oven to 400°F (200°C). Spread the almonds out in a shallow roasting pan and roast for 10–12 minutes or until lightly golden, giving them a good stir halfway through to make sure that they roast evenly. Remove from the oven, tip the almonds into a large bowl and leave to cool.

* Spread the sesame seeds out in the same pan and roast for 7–10 minutes or until golden, again stirring halfway through to make sure that they roast evenly. Remove from the oven, tip the sesame seeds into a separate bowl and leave to cool.

* Spread the flour out in the same pan and roast for 45–50 minutes or until the flour is lightly golden and turns a pale yellow, giving it a good stir every 10–15 minutes to make sure that it roasts evenly.

* While the flour is roasting, once the almonds are cool enough to handle, grind using a food processor or crush with a rolling pin until coarsely ground. Return the ground almonds to the bowl.

* Once the sesame seeds are cool enough to handle, use a food processor or a pestle and mortar to finely grind them, but make sure that you don't overgrind them, otherwise they could turn into sesame seed butter. Add the ground sesame seeds to the ground almonds in the bowl (set a small amount aside for a topping if desired), then add the aniseed, cinnamon and salt and mix together.

* As soon as the flour is ready, remove from the oven, tip the flour into the almond and sesame seed mixture and mix to combine. It's important that the flour is warm at this stage, so if you wish to finish preparing the *sellou* at a later time, reheat the flour in the oven before adding it to the other ingredients.

* Warm the honey in a microwave or in a small saucepan on the stovetop over medium heat and immediately pour it over the dry mixture. Add the butter and mix all the ingredients together to create a smooth paste. Scoop the *sellou* mixture in single tablespoonfuls and roll each into a ball. If desired, roll in the reserved ground sesame seeds and ground almonds to lightly coat.

* Leave to cool and firm up for 1 hour before serving. Store the *sellou* in an airtight container at room temperature for up to 10 days.

Funfetti gazelle horns

One thing I love about cooking, and in particular about doing this cookbook, is how it gives me the ability to bring old and new items together. The gazelle horn is one of the most symbolic pastries you will ever find in the whole Kingdom of Morocco, whereas funfetti-izing cookies is a very Western, modern baking technique. I don't know about you, but anything with colorful sprinkles always puts me in a good mood with their symbols of joy such as rainbows and unicorns. Marrying gazelle horns with sprinkles is like eating my tagine with couscous instead of the traditional bread: it's new, it's odd, but it's darn good. In order to create a visible funfetti effect, make sure that you use vibrant and colorful sprinkles.

1 ¾ cups sesame seeds
½ lb blanched almonds
½ cup superfine sugar
2 tablespoons orange blossom water
2½ teaspoons unsalted butter, softened
¼ teaspoon salt
pinch of ground cinnamon
2 tablespoons rainbow sugar sprinkles
1 egg white

* Preheat the oven to 375°F (190°C). Spread the sesame seeds out on a cookie sheet and roast for 7–10 minutes or until golden, stirring halfway through to make sure that they roast evenly. Remove from the oven, tip the sesame seeds into a shallow bowl and leave to cool. Leave the oven on at the same temperature.

* Place the almonds and sugar in a food processor with the orange blossom water, butter, salt and cinnamon and process until you have a moist paste. This will take a bit of time — about 5 minutes, depending on the machine you are using.

* Transfer the almond paste to a large bowl and stir in the sprinkles, making sure that they are evenly distributed. Divide the paste into 14 equal-sized portions, then shape each into a cylinder 2 inches long.

* Line a cookie sheet with parchment paper. Dip each almond paste cylinder into the egg white, then immediately coat in the roasted sesame seeds. Use your fingers to mold each sesame-coated cylinder into a crescent shape and place on the lined cookie sheet.

* Bake the gazelle horns for 10 minutes or until golden. Remove from the oven and leave them to cool on the cookie sheet for 10 minutes, then transfer to a wire rack to cool completely.

Pistachio, orange & olive oil flourless loaf cake

Do you know what it's like to be kissed by a cute army of smooth pistachios? If you don't, then you should bake this cake as soon as possible to remedy this unfortunate situation. Because that's how this cake's first bite will make you feel. It's dangerously addictive — so fluffy, moist and rich that it doesn't need any topping or decoration. I love to serve it for afternoon tea and as a dessert for dinner parties, and it's the perfect option for anyone who is gluten or dairy intolerant.

½ lb unsalted shelled pistachio nuts
4 large eggs, separated
½ cup olive oil, plus extra for oiling
3 tablespoons orange juice
1 tablespoon vanilla extract
⅔ cup superfine sugar
1 cup ground almonds
finely grated zest of 1 large orange
½ heaped teaspoon salt
1 teaspoon baking powder

* Preheat the oven to 375°F (190°C). Lightly oil a 2 lb loaf pan and line the base with parchment paper.

* Tip the pistachios into a food processor and pulse until ground to a flour consistency, but make sure not to overgrind them, otherwise they could turn into pistachio butter. Transfer the ground pistachios to a bowl.

* Mix the egg yolks, olive oil, orange juice and vanilla extract together in a large bowl until smooth. Add the remaining ingredients, except the egg whites, to the ground pistachios and mix together, then tip into the wet mixture and stir to combine, making sure that all the dry ingredients are moist.

* Using a hand-held electric mixer, whisk the egg whites in a separate large bowl until stiff. Gently fold into the cake mixture with a large metal spoon.

* Spread the cake mixture in the prepared pan and bake for 35–40 minutes or until the cake is golden and feels spongy to the touch, and a skewer inserted into the center of the cake comes out a little moist and sticky. Remove from the oven and leave the cake to cool in the pan for 10 minutes, then turn out, slice and serve.

Roasted almond & honey cigars

In Morocco, when sweet or savoury fillings are tucked into thin sheets of dough to form little pastries, we call them *briwate*. So officially and strictly speaking, these are roasted almond and honey *briwate*, not cigars. I have been eating them for as long as I can remember, and of all the different kinds of sweet *briwate*, these are my favorites. Serve at any time of the day with a big pot of Moroccan Mint Tea (*see* page 214).

2 cups blanched almonds
2 tablespoons olive oil
⅓ cup superfine sugar
3 tablespoons orange blossom water
½ teaspoon ground ginger
1 teaspoon ground cinnamon
½ teaspoon salt

2¾ tablespoons unsalted butter, softened
¼ cup unsalted butter, melted
7 oz filo pastry sheets
a scant cup of clear honey
freeze-dried berries or any chopped dried fruit or nuts, to decorate (optional)

* Preheat the oven to 400°F (200°C). Spread the almonds out on a cookie sheet and drizzle with the olive oil. Roast for 10–12 minutes or until lightly browned, giving the almonds a good stir halfway through to make sure that they roast evenly. Remove from the oven and leave until cool enough to handle. Keep the oven on at the same temperature.

* Tip the roasted almonds into a food processor, add the sugar, 2 tablespoons of the orange blossom water, ginger, cinnamon and salt and pulse until the almonds are finely ground. Make sure not to overgrind them, otherwise they could turn into almond butter.

* Transfer the almond mixture to a bowl, add the softened butter and mix until the ingredients are well combined and form a solid paste. Divide the almond paste into 22 equal-sized portions and shape each portion into a cylinder about 3 inches long. Cover with plastic wrap while you assemble the cigars.

* Line a cookie sheet with parchment paper. Use a sharp knife to cut the filo pastry sheets into rectangles each about 10 x 4 inches (you should end up with about 22 in total). Keep them covered

with a clean dish towel to prevent them from drying out. Lay a filo rectangle on a work surface with one shorter side closest to you and brush it with melted butter. Place an almond paste cylinder near the shorter end, leaving an equal distance (about ½ inch) clear at either end. Fold the 2 longer sides over the ends of the paste to seal it in, then start to roll up the paste tightly to create a compact cigar. Place the rolled cigar on the lined cookie sheet and brush with more melted butter. Repeat until you have used up all the almond paste cylinders. Bake for 10–12 minutes or until golden.

* Meanwhile, heat the honey in a small saucepan over medium-high heat with the remaining orange blossom water. As soon as the honey becomes foamy, reduce the heat to medium-low to avoid burning it.

* Once the cigars are ready, remove from the oven and immediately transfer them, a few at a time, to the simmering honey mixture. Leave to soak for 2–3 minutes or until golden brown, flipping them over if necessary, then use a slotted spoon to lift them out on to a rack set over greaseproof paper or a flat dish. Decorate with freeze-dried berries or any chopped dried fruits or nuts if desired, then leave to cool for 30 minutes before serving.

Ktefa — Milk bastila

If you're looking for a typical Moroccan celebratory dessert, look no further! Milk *bastila* (also known as *ktefa*) is the Moroccan equivalent of the most decadent layer cake or fine pâtisserie. It consists of layers of golden filo pastry covered in a silky crème pâtissière and roasted almonds. My brothers and I would ask our mom to make a giant one that we could eat all together. Breaking it with the back of our spoons was the best feeling ever!

¾ cup blanched almonds
1 ⅓ cup full-fat milk
3 egg yolks
3 tablespoons superfine sugar
2 tablespoons all-purpose flour
2 tablespoons cornstarch
1 ½ tablespoons clear honey

½ teaspoon orange blossom water
¼ teaspoon vanilla extract
9 oz filo pastry sheets
2¾ tablespoons unsalted butter, melted

To serve
confectioners' sugar
ground cinnamon

* Preheat the oven to 400°F (200°C). Spread the almonds out on a cookie sheet and roast for about 10–12 minutes until lightly browned, giving them a good stir halfway through to make sure that they roast evenly. Remove from the oven and leave to cool to room temperature, then grind using a food processor or crush with a rolling pin until coarsely ground. Set aside until ready to use. Leave the oven on at the same temperature.

* Now make the crème pâtissière. Heat the milk in a small saucepan over medium heat for a few minutes until it starts to simmer, then remove pan from the heat and skim off any skin that has formed on the surface.

* Mix the egg yolks, sugar, cornstarch and flour together in a large saucepan. Add a few splashes of warm milk to the egg and sugar mixture and use a whisk to stir vigorously until the mixture is smooth. Place the pan over medium heat, then gradually add the remaining warm milk, whisking constantly for 3–6 minutes or until the mixture thickens. Once it has thickened, reduce heat to low and simmer for 2 minutes, then remove pan from the heat. Stir in the honey, orange blossom water and vanilla, then transfer the crème pâtissière to a

bowl and cover the surface with plastic wrap to prevent a skin from forming. Set aside.

* Line a few cookie sheets with parchment paper. Unroll the pastry onto a work surface (keep any filo you aren't working with covered with a clean dish towel to prevent it from drying out). Using a 4 inch round cookie cutter or a saucer as a guide, cut out as many circles from the filo as possible with a sharp knife. Place as many filo circles as will fit on the lined cookie sheets, lightly brush each with melted butter and bake for about 5 minutes or until golden. Repeat until all the circles are baked.

* You can start assembling the *bastila* as soon as the filo circles have cooled to room temperature, which will only take a few minutes. The crème patissière needs to be quite warm and pourable in order to start assembling, so if it's cold and thick, warm it up in a saucepan.

* To serve, set out 6 serving plates. Place 2 filo circles on each plate, then top with 1 heaped tablespoon of crème pâtissière, 1 tablespoon roasted almonds and 2 more filo circles. Repeat the layers twice on each plate, then sprinkle the top filo circle with confectioners' sugar and ground cinnamon. Serve immediately.

Rose & almond ghriba

A cracked and cakey rose *lukum* that bursts with flavor is how I would describe these almond and rose ghribas. *Ghriba* refers to a specific type of cookie that Moroccans bake all year long. Recipes vary depending on the region or the family, but they all have one thing in common: they are cracked on the outside and chewy on the inside. When it comes to *ghriba*, the flavoring possibilities are endless, but the most popular varieties are almond, coconut and walnut.

◄━━━━►

3 cups ground almonds
⅓ cup superfine sugare
1 heaped teaspoon baking powder
½ teaspoon salt
2 tablespoons unsalted butter, softened
2 large eggs
1 teaspoon rosewater
¾ cup confectioners' sugar, for coating

◄━━━━►

* Preheat the oven to 350°F (180°C). Line a cookie sheet with parchment paper.

* Place all the ingredients, except the confectioners' sugar, in a large bowl and use your hands or a large spatula to mix them together until you have a smooth and slightly sticky dough. Scoop the dough in single tablespoonfuls and roll each into a ball, then roll each ball in confectioners' sugar until completely coated.

* Transfer the coated dough balls to the lined cookie sheet and lightly press each with the palm of your hand, but don't flatten them completely.

* Immediately bake for 15–18 minutes until the cookies are cracked and firm on the outside. Remove from the oven and leave the cookies to rest on the cookie sheet for 10 minutes before transferring them to a wire rack to cool completely. Store the cookies in an airtight container to prevent them from drying out. They will keep for up to 7 days.

Ras el hanout carrot cake with cream cheese frosting

When someone moves or travels to another country, one of the most exciting prospects is experiencing the food. Among the first things I discovered when I moved to London was carrot cake. Somehow, I had never come across this massively delicious classic. Thanks to the internet, it was easy to access a multitude of recipes, many of which I tried and then finally developed my own — this perfect, never-fail carrot cake with a Moroccan twist. My friends can't believe how simple it is to prepare and how good it tastes.

1¼ cups all-purpose flour
1½ teaspoons baking powder
1½ teaspoons baking soda
1½ teaspoons ras el hanout (*see page 9* for homemade)
1 teaspoon ground cinnamon
½ teaspoon salt
2 cups superfine sugar
¾ cup sunflower oil, plus extra for oiling

1 tablespoon vanilla extract
4 large eggs
5 oz freshly grated carrots
½ cup walnuts, chopped

Frosting
1¼ cup full-fat cream cheese
¾ cup confectioners' sugar
⅓ cup unsalted butter, softened

* Preheat the oven to 375°F (190°C). Oil an 8 inch deep round cake pan, then line with parchment paper.

* Mix the flour, baking powder, baking soda, ras el hanout, cinammon and salt together in a large bowl. Place the sugar, oil, vanilla extract and eggs in a separate large bowl and stir together with a whisk or fork until well blended.

* Add the flour mixture to the egg and sugar mixture and stir just to combine — be careful not to overmix as this will make the cake too dense. Then add the grated carrots and walnuts and stir to combine.

* Pour the cake mixture into the prepared cake pan and bake for 35–40 minutes until the top is golden brown, the cake feels spongy to the touch and a skewer inserted into the center comes out dry.

* Meanwhile, make the frosting. Place all the ingredients in a large bowl and use a hand-held electric mixer to slowly beat them together until smooth and fluffy. Cover the bowl with plastic wrap and keep in the fridge until ready to use.

* Remove the cake from the oven and leave to cool in the pan for 10 minutes, then transfer from the pan to a wire rack to finish cooling. Once your cake is completely cool, cover the top with the frosting and serve.

Jabane — Nougat

When I was little, my mom loved to drag me around everywhere, especially the souk where she could practice some of her favorite activities — bargaining and buying food. The bargaining part always embarrassed me until I started trying it out myself — like mother, like daughter! Back then, my mom had one essential rule for me: never to let go of her hand. The best bit about obeying this rule was that at the end of the day she would reward me with a generous piece of *jabane*. *Jabane* is to Morocco what *turrón* is to Spain, *torrone* is to Italy and Nougat de Montélimar is to France. Going to the *jabane* stand and choosing a piece of soft and chewy nougat was definitely *my* favorite part of the souk excursion.

⅓ cup unsalted shelled pistachio nuts
⅓ cup blanched hazelnuts
cornstarch, for dusting
1 large egg white
pinch of salt
1 ¼ cup superfine sugar

3 tablespoons corn syrup
¼ cup clear honey
¼ cup water
½ teaspoon orange blossom water
⅛ teaspoon almond extract
⅓ cup dried cranberries

* Preheat the oven to 400°F (200°C). Spread the pistachios and hazelnuts out on a cookie sheet and roast for 6–8 minutes until lightly browned, giving the nuts a good stir halfway through to make sure that they roast evenly. Remove from the oven and set aside until ready to use.

* Cut 2 sheets of parchment paper each about 12 inches long and lightly dust each of them with cornstarch. Set aside for spreading out the *jabane* mixture later on.

* Place the egg white in a large heatproof bowl with the salt and have a hand-held electric mixer at the ready. Alternatively, place the egg white and salt in the bowl of a stand mixer fitted with the whisk attachment.

* Combine the sugar, corn syrup, honey and water in a saucepan over low heat and use a spatula to stir the mixture, making sure it doesn't touch the edges of the pan (this will help prevent the sugar from crystallizing). Increase the heat to medium, add a sugar thermometer to the pan and monitor the heat until it reaches 275°F (135°C). It will take a bit of time for the mixture to reach this temperature, but don't be tempted to increase the

heat to speed up the process because it is likely to burn. As soon as the mixture reaches 275°F (135°C), whisk the egg white until stiff, while continuing to heat the sugar and honey mixture. When the mixture reaches 350°F (150°C), immediately remove pan from the heat and pour the hot syrup into the whisked egg white as you continue whisking on a low speed. Once all the syrup has been added to the whisked egg white, add the orange blossom water and almond extract, increase the speed and whisk for about 6 minutes until the mixture becomes thick and heavy.

* Add the roasted nuts and cranberries to the mixture, using a large spatula to vigorously mix them in. Dust the spatula with cornstarch and use it to scoop out and spread the mixture evenly over one of the prepared parchment paper sheets. Cover with the other sheet, pressing down with your hands to level the surface. Then roll over the top sheet with a rolling pin to ensure that you have an even layer of mixture.

* Leave to cool at room temperature for about 4 hours until firm. Peel off the parchment paper and cut the *jabane* into pieces of your desired size.

Chebakia sugar cookies

Chebakia, also known as *mkharka*, *griwech* or *rose des sables*, is a wonderfully fragrant cookie usually enjoyed in Moroccan households during the month of Ramadan. Its preparation is a little bit complex and requires quite a lot of time, so when I have a craving for *chebakia*, I usually *chebakia*-ize my favorite cookies in the whole wide world — sugar cookies! Sugar cookies are so simple and yet so adaptable. When prepared the right way and with the right ingredients, they have the ability to lead you to an enchanted food paradise. So here is my *chebakia*-ized sugar cookie: half sugar cookie, half *chebakia* and a full hybrid of my cravings and laziness.

4 tablespoons sesame seeds
1 cup unsalted butter, softened
⅔ cup superfine sugar
¾ cup soft light brown sugar
2 large eggs
4 tablespoons clear honey
2 tablespoons orange blossom water

3½ cups all-purpose flour
1 teaspoon baking soda
1 teaspoon baking powder
1 teaspoon salt
½ teaspoon ground cinnamon
½ teaspoon ground aniseed
½ teaspoon ground turmeric

* Heat a small saucepan over medium heat, add the sesame seeds and toast for about 3 minutes until golden brown, tossing occasionally. Set aside.

* Cream the butter and sugars together in a large bowl with a hand-held electric mixer or using a stand mixer fitted with the paddle attachment for about 2–3 minutes or until the mixture is smooth and turns a pale beige color. Add the eggs, honey and orange blossom water and beat again until well combined. Add the flour, toasted sesame seeds, baking soda, baking powder, salt and spices and mix on a low speed until everything is incorporated — be careful not to overmix as this will make the cookies quite tough. Cover the dough with plastic wrap and leave to rest in the fridge for a minimum of 2 and up to 24 hours.

* When ready to bake, preheat the oven to 375°F (190°C). Line a cookie sheet with parchment paper.

* Scoop the dough in single tablespoonfuls and roll each into a ball. Place the cookies on the lined cookie sheet, leaving at least 2 inches between each of them, and bake for about 10 minutes until the edges are lightly golden brown and the center is a bit soft. Remove from the oven and leave the cookies to rest on the sheet for 5 minutes, then transfer them to a wire rack to cool completely — if you try to remove them sooner, you may damage the cookies.

Roasted grape & pistachio saykouk — Buttermilk & couscous porridge

In Morocco, *saykouk* refers to cooked couscous mixed with cold buttermilk. Typically enjoyed for breakfast or as a refreshing snack, it is often served in the summer. As a child I was not a big fan, and the only way for me to finish my bowl of *saykouk* was with plenty of (and probably way too much) honey. Thankfully, while growing up, my palate evolved and I came up with a better way to enjoy *saykouk*: with roasted grapes and pistachios. I think of it as a fancy breakfast bowl or a quick dessert.

3 tablespoons orange blossom water
2 tablespoons clear honey,
plus extra to serve (optional)
2 tablespoons olive oil
pinch of salt

1 lb 12 oz red grapes
1 ¼ cups wholewheat couscous, cooked
according to the packet instructions
2 cups buttermilk
⅓ cup unsalted shelled pistachio nuts,
roughly chopped

* Preheat the oven to 430°F (220°C). Mix the orange blossom water, honey, olive oil and salt together in a large bowl. Add the grapes and lightly toss to coat in the mixture. Transfer the grapes to a cookie sheet and roast for about 15 minutes until they are wrinkly and soft.

* To serve, divide the cooked couscous between 4 shallow bowls and pour in some buttermilk — just enough to cover the couscous. Top with the roasted grapes and pistachios and, finally, drizzle with extra honey if desired. Serve immediately.

Moroccan mint tea

Moroccans drink their tea pretty much at any time of the day: for breakfast with *baghrir* (*see* page 44) and Almond *Msemen* (*see* page 178), in the afternoon with Funfetti Gazelle Horns (*see* page 197) or Rose & Almond *Ghriba* (*see* page 204) and after a comforting meal. Its sweet taste and refreshing virtues are indeed quite special, although the only specialist ingredient you need in order to make proper Moroccan mint tea is gunpowder tea. This is a type of green Chinese tea in which each leaf has been rolled into a small pellet — you will find it online or in Middle Eastern grocery shops. You can flavor your Moroccan tea with any other aromatic fresh herb if you like, such as lemon verbena, sage or geranium, or even rose petals. To make authentic Moroccan tea, you will also need a traditional Moroccan teapot, or a kettle — one that you can safely use on your stovetop — and a tea strainer for straining your tea as you pour it.

1 heaped teaspoon loose leaf gunpowder green tea
2½ cups boiling water
8 mint sprigs, plus extra to serve
1–3 tablespoons superfine sugar, or more to taste

* Add the gunpowder tea and ½ cup of the boiling water to a Moroccan teapot or stovetop kettle and simmer over medium heat for 1 minute. Pour the water out into a cup; if using a stove-top kettle, strain the water through a tea strainer and return the tea leaves to the kettle. Set the cup of water aside — don't discard it, as it contains the essence of the tea.

* Pour another ½ cup of the boiling water into the teapot or kettle, but this time swirl the pot or kettle a couple times to rinse the tea leaves. Pour the water out and discard it, but again strain the water if using a stovetop kettle and return the tea leaves to the kettle.

* Add the mint, 1 tablespoon of sugar and reserved cup of water to the teapot or kettle. Fill with the remaining boiling water and simmer gently over low heat for about 5 minutes until it comes to a boil. It's important to let the tea come to a boil slowly to allow the tea leaves and mint to steep properly. If you are using a Moroccan teapot, you will see steam coming out of the pot once it comes to a boil.

* Carefully open the teapot or kettle and, using a large spoon, stir the tea to make sure that the sugar is well dissolved. Taste and add more sugar if desired. Serve immediately. If using a stovetop kettle, strain the tea when pouring and discard the tea leaves. Serve with a sprig of fresh mint.

Moroccan mint tea chocolate pots

Chocolate we adore; Moroccan mint tea we love. What is there left to say about these little pots of happiness, as I like to call them? Except to mention that every time I serve these, all are amazed by their creamy chocolaty quality while at the same time having a subtle taste of Moroccan mint tea. So this dessert definitely manages to capture the best of both worlds. If desired, enjoy your chocolate pot with a dollop of whipped cream or a serving of custard.

1 cup heavy cream

1½ tablespoons unsalted butter

3 teaspoons loose leaf gunpowder green tea

handful of mint leaves

1½ cups dark chocolate (70% cocoa solids), roughly chopped

½ teaspoon vanilla extract

⅓ cup superfine sugar

3 large egg yolks

pinch of salt

* Heat the cream with the butter in a small saucepan over medium heat until it comes to a boil. Remove the pan from the heat and stir in the gunpowder tea and mint leaves. Leave to steep for 30 minutes.

* Strain the cream and butter mixture thoroughly, discarding the tea and mint leaves, return to the saucepan and set over medium-low heat. Add the chocolate and vanilla and heat for about 4 minutes, stirring, until the chocolate has melted and the mixture is smooth. Remove the pan from the heat and leave the mixture to cool for a few minutes.

* Whisk the sugar, egg yolks and salt together in a large bowl using a hand-held electric mixer until pale in color. Pour in the chocolate mixture while stirring constantly and continue stirring until smooth and well combined.

* Divide the mixture between 4 small pots or ramekins and chill in the fridge for about 1 hour until firm. If you keep the pots in the fridge for more than 2 hours, leave them at room temperature for 30 minutes before serving.

Index

Acknowledgments

My wonderful adventure with food started with my blog mymoroccanfood.com right after I finished my cookery training at Leith's. Launching my blog required some courage and massive support from my family and friends. To those who encouraged me to pursue my passion and who persistently believed in my career move, I am eternally grateful for your support.

To the readers of my blog, your encouragement has played an immense role in keeping me motivated to post recipes and remain creative these past years. I probably would never have had a book deal if you hadn't tried so many of my recipes and sent me positive feedback. This book is for you.

To Stephanie Jackson, my publisher, who agreed to meet with me when I was agent-less and at a time when the cookery book market is incredibly competitive. My husband will never forget how loud I screamed with joy when I received your answer to my email. I am sincerely grateful for that and for commissioning me as one of your authors.

To Ariella Feiner, for her steady support and giving me detailed and honest advice from the very beginning, when I was working on my proposal until the very end of the book-writing process. I am glad to call you my agent.

A huge thank you to Sybella Stephens and Juliette Norsworthy for being patiently involved in so many creative aspects of my book, and for translating my vision and my words into something beautiful which I am proud of.

A big thank you to Matt Russell for not only capturing my recipes with beauty but also doing it smoothly and pleasantly during the intense and long days of the photoshoot. In the same way, I'd like to thank Aya Nishimura for cooking a dozen recipes a day, remaining calm and managing to make them look effortlessly natural and stunning. To the rest of the talented creative team behind *Casablanca*: Lydia McPherson, Aya's assistant Nicola Roberts and Matt's assistant Stephanie Howard, thank you for your hard work.

To my mom, who taught me how to cook effortlessly for 5 or 12 people and for showing me how cooking should never be a task but something we do out of love and for the people we love. Thank you for always answering the phone when I am stuck with a recipe and for giving me countless cooking tricks and advice. I love you, Mama.

To my father, who taught me how to value quality over quantity when it comes to food and for prompting me to appreciate fresh and seasonal products while growing up. Thank you for showing me all these years that good is not enough when great is possible and how dedication always pays off.

To my husband, Zayd. You've believed in me and in this book more than I did and it certainly wouldn't exist without you. Thank you for your absolute support throughout this journey, especially when I had doubts and felt lost. You inspire me every day to work hard and to always look on the bright side but above all, you inspire me to unapologetically be me, with others and mainly with myself.
Your love is magic and you are my hero.